CAMBRIDGE PRIMARY
Mathematics
Learner's Book

4

Emma Low

CAMBRIDGE
UNIVERSITY PRESS

CAMBRIDGE
UNIVERSITY PRESS

University Printing House, Cambridge CB2 8BS, United Kingdom

Cambridge University Press is part of the University of Cambridge.

It furthers the University's mission by disseminating knowledge in the pursuit of education, learning and research at the highest international levels of excellence.

www.cambridge.org
Information on this title: www.cambridge.org/9781107662698

© Cambridge University Press 2014

First published 2014

Printed in the United Kingdom by Latimer Trend

A catalogue record for this publication is available from the British Library

ISBN 978-1-107-66269-8 Paperback

Cover artwork by Bill Bolton

....

Introduction

This *Learner's Book* is a supplementary resource that consolidates and reinforces mathematical learning alongside the *Cambridge Primary Mathematics Teacher's Resource 4* (9781107692947). It provides introductory investigations (Let's investigate) to encourage the application of mathematical knowledge, and numerous questions and activities to develop problem-solving skills.

Ideally, a session should be taught using the appropriate *Core activity* in the *Teacher's Resource 4*. The associated content in the *Learner's Book 4* can then be used for formative assessment at the end of a session, for homework, or used for support in learning new vocabulary. There is generally a double page corresponding to each *Core activity* in the *Teacher's Resource 4* printed book. The *Core activity* that the page relates to is indicated at the bottom of the page.

Hints and tips are provided throughout to support the learners. They will appear as follows:

Write a list of number pairs to help you

Please note that the *Learner's Book* on its own does **not** cover all of the Cambridge Primary mathematics curriculum framework for Stage 4. You need to use it in conjunction with the *Teacher's Resource 4* to ensure full coverage.

This publication is part of the *Cambridge Primary Maths* project. *Cambridge Primary Maths* is an innovative combination of curriculum and resources designed to support teachers and learners to succeed in primary mathematics through best-practice international maths teaching and a problem-solving approach.

Cambridge Primary Maths brings together the world-class Cambridge Primary mathematics curriculum from Cambridge International Examinations, high-quality publishing from Cambridge University Press and expertise in engaging online enrichment materials for the mathematics curriculum from NRICH.

Teachers have access to an online tool that maps resources and links to materials offered through the primary mathematics curriculum, NRICH and Cambridge Primary mathematics textbooks and e-books. These resources include engaging online activities, best-practice guidance and examples of *Cambridge Primary Maths* in action.

The Cambridge curriculum is dedicated to helping schools develop learners who are confident, responsible, reflective, innovative and engaged. It is designed to give learners the skills to problem solve effectively, apply mathematical knowledge and develop a holistic understanding of the subject.

The *Cambridge Primary Maths* textbooks provide best-in-class support for this problem-solving approach, based on pedagogical practice found in successful schools across the world. The engaging NRICH online resources help develop mathematical thinking and problem-solving skills. To get involved visit www.cie.org.uk/cambridgeprimarymaths

The benefits of being part of *Cambridge Primary Maths* are:
- the opportunity to explore a maths curriculum founded on the values of the University of Cambridge and best practice in schools
- access to an innovative package of online and print resources that can help bring the Cambridge Primary mathematics curriculum to life in the classroom.

This series is arranged to ensure that the curriculum is covered whilst allowing teachers to use a flexible approach. The Scheme of Work for Stage 4 has been followed, though not in the same order and there will be some deviations. The components are:
- Teacher's Resource 4
  ISBN: 9781107692947 (printed book and CD-ROM).
- Learner's Book 4
  ISBN: 9781107662698 (printed book)
- Games Book 4
  ISBN: 9781107685420 (printed book and CD-ROM).

For associated NRICH activities, please visit the *Cambridge Primary Maths* project at www.cie.org.uk/cambridgeprimarymaths

Number

Reading, writing and partitioning numbers

Let's investigate

Pablo has these digit cards.

He makes three-digit numbers with the cards.

Write down all the numbers he could make.

1 Write each **red** number in **figures**, **words** and **expanded form**.

(a)

1000	2000	**3000**	4000	5000	6000	7000	8000	9000
100	200	300	400	**500**	600	700	800	900
10	20	30	40	50	60	**70**	80	90
1	2	3	4	5	6	7	8	9

(b)

1000	2000	3000	4000	5000	6000	7000	8000	9000
100	200	300	400	500	600	700	800	**900**
10	20	30	40	50	60	70	80	90
1	2	3	4	5	6	7	8	**9**

2 Write each number in words.

(a) 2345 (b) 3030 (c) 2901

(d) 7777 (e) 2816 (f) 9109

3 Write these numbers in figures.

(a) nine thousand and nine

(b) four thousand and forty

4 What is the value of 4 in these numbers?

(a) 6423 (b) 4623 (c) 3409

(d) 9040 (e) 1234 (f) 4321

Vocabulary

digit: 0, 1, 2, 3, 4, 5, 6, 7, 8 and 9 are digits.

expanded form: 4567 = 4000 + 500 + 60 + 7

partition: breaking up a number into its parts.

place value: the value of a digit determined by its position.

In 830, the 3 has a value of 3 tens (30).

H	T	U
8	3	0

thousand: is a four-digit number that is 10 times larger than a hundred.

Th	H	T	U
1	0	0	0

×10

5 Look at these number cards.

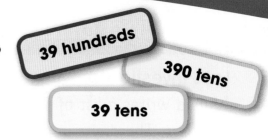

(a) Which cards have the same value as 3900?

(b) Which card has the smallest value?

(c) What is 10 more than 390 tens?

6 Maria writes a number. It has the digit 4 in the hundreds place and the digit 2 in the units place.
Which of these numbers could Maria have written?

5426   4652   4265   5462

7 What is the largest possible number that can be written using the digits 3, 6, 3 and 4?

8 Which value is equal to 3 hundreds?

3 units   30 units   30 tens   300 tens

9 Find the missing numbers.

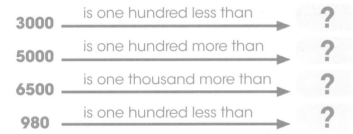

10 Write the number that is 1 more than 9999.

11 Solve these number riddles.

(a) • I have four digits.
     • I am more than 2500.
     • I am less than 3000.
     • My hundreds digit is 6.
     • My tens digit is one less than my hundreds digit.
     • My units digit is 0.
     What number am I?

(b) • I have four digits.
     • My units digit and my hundreds digit are the same.
     • I am less than 9000.
     • I am greater than 8000.
     • My tens digit is 4.
     • My hundreds digit is two more than my tens digit.
     What number am I?

Ordering and rounding

Let's investigate

Ahmed writes a list of four-digit whole numbers. The digits in each number add up to 3.

$1+0+2+0=3$

1020

He writes the numbers in order of size, starting with the smallest.
Write down all the numbers that could be in Ahmed's list. Make sure you write them in order of size.

Vocabulary

round to the nearest: to round to the nearest **hundred**, look at the **tens** digit and if it is

H	T	U
8	?	0

• < 5, *round down* ⬇

• $= 5$ or > 5, *round up* ⬆

H	T	U
8	3	0

830 to the nearest **hundred**, is 800.

H	T	U
	4	8

48 to the nearest **ten**, is 50.

Rounding numbers makes them easier to use.

---

1 Write these numbers in order of size, starting with the smallest.

   (a) 1066   1606   1660   1060   1666

   (b) 9080   8990   9009   9090   8999

2 What is the number shown by an arrow on each number line?

   (a)

   (b)

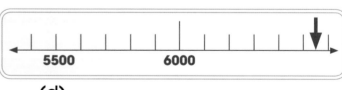

   (c)

   (d)

3 Round these numbers to the nearest 100.

   (a) 1060   (b) 7225   (c) 4680   (d) 1007   (e) 885

4 Which of these numbers is closest to 1000?

   1050   1039   1100   980   899

5 Here are some digit cards.

Use the cards to make three-digit numbers **greater than** 500.
How many can you make?

6 Use the < and > signs to make these statements true.

(a) 505 **?** 550   (b) 660 **?** 606   (c) 989 **?** 899

(d) 1234 **?** 4321   (e) 1009 **?** 1010   (f) 1001 **?** 989

7 What number is halfway between 158 and 172?

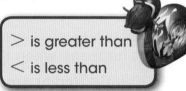

> is greater than
< is less than

158 ———— **?** ———— **172**

8 Find the numbers halfway between these pairs of numbers.

(a) 498 and 604   (b) 337 and 451   (c) 559 and 997

9 Here are four numbers: 3005   3006   3007   3009

Choose one number to make this number sentence correct.

3007 < **?**

10 Which of these numbers is **about** the same size as the correct answer to 480 + 490?

100   500   400

1000   700   2000

11 Here are five digits.

Choose three of these digits to make the total as close as possible to 1000.

300 + **?** **?** **?** = **?**

Multiplying and dividing by 10 and 100

Let's investigate

Use a calculator. Key in these numbers and signs.

$$5 \times 10 = = = \ldots$$

$$11 \times 100 = = = \ldots$$

$$12\,500 \div 10 = = = \ldots$$

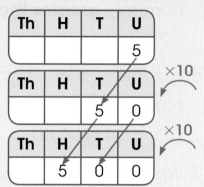

What happens when you press the equals (=) sign?

Try using different start numbers. Do you notice the same thing?

1   Calculate.

(a) 67×10 (b) $40 \div 10$ (c) $3600 \div 100$

(d) 415×10 (e) $350 \div 10$ (f) 35×100

(g) $4100 \div 100$ (h) $4700 \div 10$ (i) $3900 \div 100$

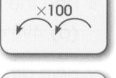

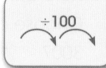

2   What is the missing number? $5400 \div \boxed{?}\ \boxed{?} = 100$

3   Write the missing digits.

(a) $\boxed{?}\ \boxed{?}\ \boxed{?} \times 10 = 2320$ (b) $461\ \boxed{?} \div 10 = \boxed{?}\ 61$

(c) $34\ \boxed{?}\ 0 \div 10 = \boxed{?}\ \boxed{?}\ 6$ (d) $31\ \boxed{?} \times 10 = \boxed{?}\ \boxed{?}\ 60$

4   Write the missing numbers.

(a) $\boxed{?} \div 10 = 54$ (b) $307 \times \boxed{?} = 3070$

(c) $\boxed{?} \times 100 = 6000$ (d) $3400 \div \boxed{?} = 34$

5   Here are four number cards.

A fifty-eight

B five hundred and eighty

C eight hundred and fifty

D five hundred and eight

Write down the letter of the card that is the answer to:

(a) 85×10 (b) $5800 \div 10$ (c) $5800 \div 100$

(d) $8500 \div 10$ (e) $580 \div 10$ (f) $5080 \div 10$

6 Calculate.

(a) $3800 \text{ cm} = \boxed{?} \text{ m}$ (b) $64 \text{ m} = \boxed{?} \text{ cm}$

(c) $500 \text{ mm} = \boxed{?} \text{ cm}$ (d) $\boxed{?} \text{ mm} = 67 \text{ cm}$

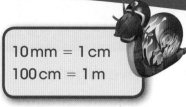

> $10 \text{ mm} = 1 \text{ cm}$
> $100 \text{ cm} = 1 \text{ m}$

7 Copy the diagrams below. Write down the missing numbers.

(a)

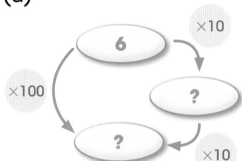

(b)

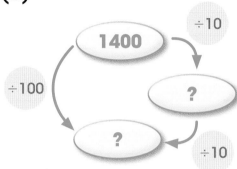

(c)

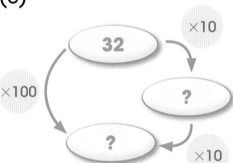

(d)

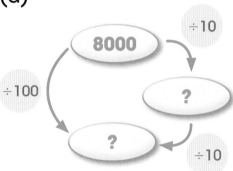

8 Here is a number calculation. $15 \times 10 = 150$

Write two different division calculations that use the same numbers.

9 A packet contains 500 grams of gerbil food.
Aysha feeds her gerbil 10 grams of food each day.
How many days does the packet of food last?

10 Here are three signs $\times$ $\div$ $=$

Use these signs to make each calculation below correct.
There may be more than one answer.

(a) $60 \boxed{?} 6 \boxed{?} 10$ (b) $10 \boxed{?} 15 \boxed{?} 150$ (c) $450 \boxed{?} 10 \boxed{?} 45$

11 Write the missing numbers.

$13 \xrightarrow{\times 10} \boxed{?} \xrightarrow{\times 10} \boxed{?}$ $4500 \xrightarrow{\div 10} \boxed{?} \xrightarrow{\div 10} \boxed{?}$

Addition (1)

Let's investigate

Make a route through the grid from Start to Finish. You can move horizontally or vertically. Add up the numbers on your route. Find the route that gives the **lowest** total.

4	8	2	Finish
9	1	4	6
8	5	5	2
2	4	3	8
Start	1	7	9

For example, $2 + 8 + 5 + 1 + 9 + 4 + 8 + 2 = 34$

Some words that we use for addition: add, addition, plus, increase, sum, total, altogether.

Questions that ask us to add: How many are there altogether? What is the total number of ...?

1 Choose a method to solve these addition problems.

(a) $5 + 8 + 5 + 3 =$? (b) $4 + 19 + 12 + 1 =$?

(c) $1 + 11 + 9 + 4 =$? (d) $4 + 17 + 2 + 3 =$?

(e) $13 + 2 + 1 + 5 =$? (f) $3 + 14 + 9 + 3 =$?

Use complements to 10 and 20 to help you. These are also called 'number pairs' to 10 and 20.

Explain to your partner why you chose that method. If you think your partner could choose a better method, tell them why.

2 Copy the addition number sentences below. Then copy the list of numbers on the right. Draw arrows to complete the number sentences. The first one has been done for you.

$76 + 52 =$	168
$28 + 34 =$	85
$65 + 89 =$	128
$94 + 22 =$	154
$17 + 68 =$	104
$43 + 52 =$	95
$91 + 77 =$	62
$40 + 64 =$	116

3 Throw hoops over the cones to make the totals in the stars.
All four hoops must land on a cone.
There can be more than one hoop on a cone.

Check your total is correct by adding together your
numbers using two different methods.

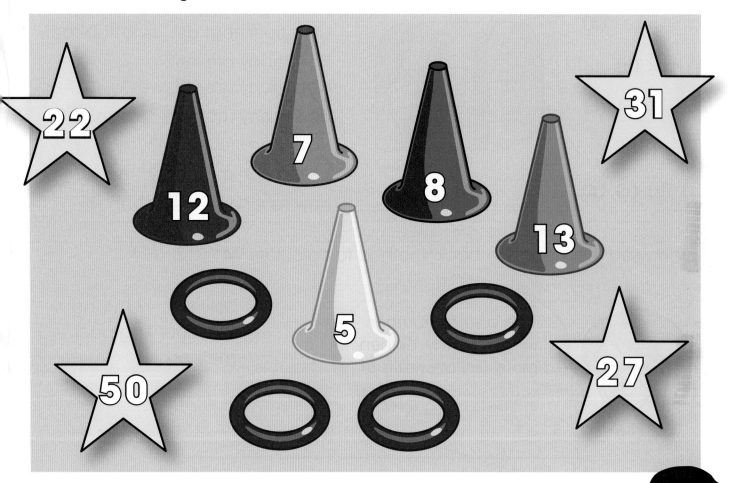

4 Number sentence stories

Kasim thought up a story for the number sentence

$63 + 56 = 119$.

Write a story for each of these number sentences:

$16 + 8 + 4 = 28$

$5 + 4 + 6 + 5 = 20$

$49 + 37 = 86$

63 people visited our art show on Monday and 56 visited on Tuesday. So 119 people visited our art show altogether.

Subtraction (1)

Let's investigate

Break the four-digit code to open the treasure chest.

$65 - 58 =$ **(a)**

$41 - 2$ **(b)** $= 12$

$86 - 79 =$ **(c)**

$67 -$ **(d)** $8 = 39$

(a) (b) (c) (d)

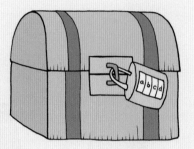

Sarah used the 'counting back' method to calculate $74 - 13$.

13 is a small number.
I will take away 10 then
3 more. The answer is 61.

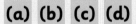

1 Solve $62 - 11$ using the 'counting back' method.

Tim used 'finding the difference' to calculate $81 - 76$.

76 is quite close to 81.
I will count up to find the difference between the numbers.
The answer is 5.

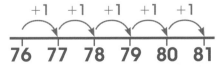

2 Solve $62 - 58$ by 'finding the difference' between the two numbers.

3 Choose a method to solve these subtraction problems.

(a) 45 − 43 = ?   (b) 92 − 14 = ?   (c) 36 − 29 = ?

(d) 89 − 5 = ?   (e) 52 − 34 = ?   (f) 42 − 18 = ?

(g) 77 − 68 = ?   (h) 39 − 35 = ?

Explain to your partner why you used your chosen methods.
If you think your partner could choose a better method, tell them why.

4 Fred leaves his house with 99 cents and walks to the shop.
He needs 15 cents to buy a snack. But Fred has a hole in his pocket!
Each time he passes a ☆, Fred loses that amount of money from his
pocket. This map shows all the possible routes from his home to the shop.

Find Fred a route to the shop so that he will still have enough money
to buy his snack when he gets there.

5 Number sentence stories

Hayley thought up a story for 86 − 49 = 37.

Write a story for each of these number sentences.

35 − 7 = 28

77 − 68 = 9

95 − 35 = 60

A shop had 86
loaves of bread. They sold
49 loaves, so 37 were left.

Partitioning to add and subtract

Let's investigate

Find five pairs of numbers that add up to 900.
One has been done for you.

$672 + 228 = 900$

545	238	86	228
96	791	355	601
672	109	589	437
463	322	814	465

Vocabulary

partition: breaking up a number into parts.
For example,
$608 = 600 + 8$.

900 is a multiple of 10. Look for two numbers that add to make a multiple of 10. We can do this by looking for number pairs to 10 in the units digits. Then choose a method to add the two numbers together.

For example, 67 **2** + 22 **8** ...

Partitioning to add

$423 + 589 =$ **?**

$400 + 20 + 3$ add $500 + 80 + 9$

$400 + 500 = 900$
$20 + 80 = 100$
$3 + 9 = 12$

Therefore, $423 + 589 = 1012$

---

1 Partition each number into hundreds, tens and ones.
   Then calculate each answer.

   (a) $482 + 213 =$ **?**

   (b) $237 + 149 =$ **?**

   (c) $821 + 546 =$ **?**

   (d) $271 + 649 =$ **?**

   (e) $362 + 841 =$ **?**

   (f) $598 + 613 =$ **?**

Partitioning to subtract

$623 - 238 = ?$

$500 + 110 + 13 - 200 + 30 + 8$

$500 - 200 = 300$
$110 - 30 = 80$
$13 - 8 = 5$

Therefore, $623 - 238 = 385$

2   Partition each number into hundreds, tens and ones.
    Then calculate each answer.

(a) $628 - 405 = ?$

(b) $972 - 813 = ?$

(c) $716 - 246 = ?$

(d) $609 - 388 = ?$

(e) $981 - 458 = ?$

(f) $560 - 308 = ?$

(g) $612 - 237 = ?$

(h) $507 - 239 = ?$

> If we partition 623 to $600 + 20 + 3$, then later we will have to calculate $20 - 30$ and $3 - 8$. So, we partition it to $500 + 110 + 13$.

3   Choose a method to solve each of these problems.
    Explain why you used your chosen methods.

(a) I bought a television for $438 and the delivery charge was $48.
    How much did I pay altogether?

(b) A sea journey is 657 km. So far the ship has travelled 239 km.
    How much further does the ship have to travel?

(c) I bought 350 beads. I used 124 beads to make jewellery
    for my friends.
    How many beads do I have left?

(d) My tree grew 68 cm one year, then 57 cm the next year,
    and 72 cm the year after that.
    How much has it grown in total over the 3 years?

Learning multiplication facts

Let's investigate

Try to learn multiplication facts for the 2×, 3×, 4×, 5×, 6×, 9× and 10× tables so you can remember them quickly. For example:

- ×2 multiples are **even** numbers
- ×5 multiples end in **0** or **5**
- ×10 multiples end in **0**.

1 Use a blank multiplication square like the one here to look for patterns.

×	1	2	3	4	5	6	7	8	9	10
1				R	O	W				
2										
3	C									
4	O									
5	L									
6	U									
7	M									
8	N									
9										
10										

multiple: a number that can be divided exactly by another number is a multiple of that number. Start at 0 and count up in steps of the same size and you will find numbers that are multiples of the step size.

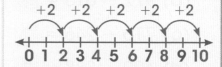

So the multiples of 2 are 2, 4, 6, 8, 10, 12 …

The multiples of 3 are 3, 6, 9, 12 …

(a) Write the 1× table across the first row and down the first column. The table is symmetrical so the answers in the first column will be the same as the answers in the first row:

1 × 2 = 2 (row) and 2 × 1 = 2 (column)

(b) Repeat for other times tables such as the 2×, 5× and 10× tables.

(c) Look at the blank squares. Think about how you could fill them in.

You could use:
- Counting on or repeated addition. You already have the first two multiples of 3 (3 and 6) so keep adding 3 to give you 9, 12, 15.
- Using existing answers. You already have answers for the 2× table, so multiply each answer by 2 to give you the 4× table. Then multiply the answers to the 4× table by two to get the 8× table.

Complete the rest of the multiplication grid.

2 Look at the spider diagrams for the 2× table.
Copy the diagrams and fill in the missing boxes.

(a)

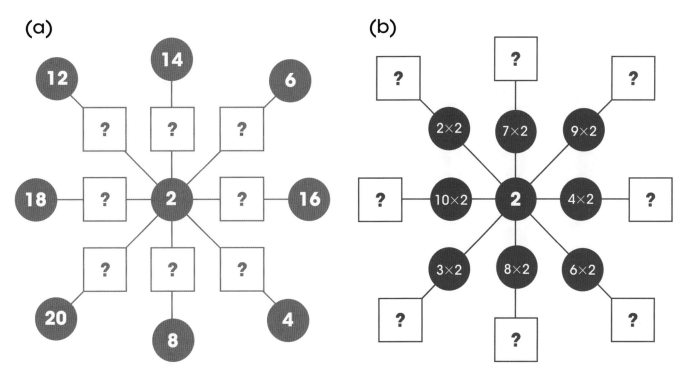

(b)

Work with a partner to create spider diagrams for other times tables.

3 Look at the numbers in the two circles.

Find pairs of numbers in the first circle that multiply together to give an answer from inside the second circle.

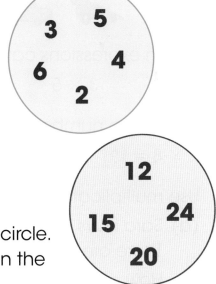

Find as many pairs of numbers as possible.
Record both multiplications for each pair.
For example: $5 \times 4 = 20$ and $4 \times 5 = 20$

Work with a partner. Draw two circles each.
Choose five numbers from 1 to 9 to write in one circle.
Swap circles and work out the answers to write in the second circle.
Ask your partner to check your work.

Using multiplication facts

Let's investigate

What number goes in the circle to complete the puzzle?

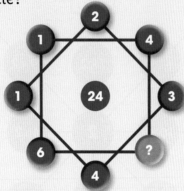

Vocabulary

expression: numbers and signs grouped to show how much something is. For example, 4 + 2 is an expression for 6, and 3 × 5 is an expression for 15.

product: the answer you get when you multiply numbers.

3 × 5 = (15) ⟵——— product

inverse: signs that 'undo' each other. Multiply and divide are inverse signs, for example,

×5

7   **35**

÷5

1 Sanjiv has a collection of toy cars.

Which expressions can he use to find the total number of toy cars?

5×3 3×5 $3 + 3 + 3$ $5 \times 5 \times 5$

2 Which two number sentences have the same answer?

$2 \times 8 =$ **?** $2 \times 9 =$ **?** $3 \times 7 =$ **?** $4 \times 4 =$ **?**

3 Use multiplication facts to help you answer these questions.

(a) Sara buys 3 bunches of bananas.
There are 6 bananas in each bunch.
How many bananas does Sara buy altogether?

(b) Ahmed paints 4 rows of animals. He paints 8 animals in each row.
What is the total number of animals Ahmed paints?

(c) Fatima has 5 packets of beads. Each packet contains 8 beads.
How many beads has Fatima got?

4   Use each of the digits 3, 5, 7 and 0 to complete these statements.
    You can only use each digit once.

    ? **?** is a multiple of 5 greater than 50.

    ? **?** is a multiple of 10 less than 50.

5   Hugo is thinking of a number.

    He says: 'My number is a multiple of 2 and a multiple of 3.
    My number is greater than 10.'

    What is the smallest number Hugo could be thinking of?

6   Which numbers on the grid are multiples of 5?

61	62	63	64	65
69	70	71	72	73
77	78	79	80	81

7   Parveen has some number cards.

    (a) She says: 'If I multiply the number on my card by 5 the answer is 45.'
    What number is on her card?

    (b) She chooses a different card and says:
    'If I divide the number on this card by 4 the answer is 6.'
    What number is on her card?

    (c) Write some similar puzzles for your partner to try.

8   Find the missing numbers.

    (a) $4 \times 5 =$ **?**   **(b)** $5 \times$ **?** $= 45$ **(c)** **?** $\times 3 = 27$

9   Look at this list of numbers. Which ones are multiples of 3?

    23   12   21   27   26   9

    28   22   15   17   18

    Look at your answers. Explain to your partner what you notice about them.

Investigating patterns

Work through these investigations with a partner.

1　These triangles are made from sticks.

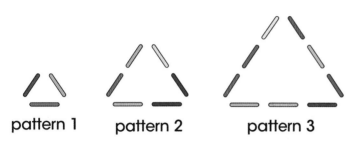

pattern 1　　pattern 2　　pattern 3

Pattern number	Number of sticks
1	3
2	6
3	9

(a) How many sticks would be needed to make pattern 7?

(b) How many sticks would be needed to make pattern 17?

(c) Which pattern could be made from 33 sticks?

2　These squares are made from sticks.

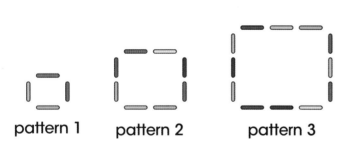

pattern 1　　pattern 2　　pattern 3

Pattern number	Number of sticks
1	4
2	8
3	12

(a) How many sticks would be needed to make pattern 9?

(b) How many sticks would be needed to make pattern 15?

(c) Which pattern could be made from 48 sticks? How do you know?
　　Explain to your partner how you worked out the answer.

3 Look at these stair patterns.

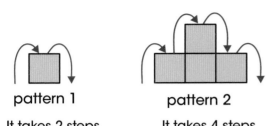 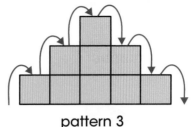

pattern 1

It takes 2 steps
to go up and down.

pattern 2

It takes 4 steps
to go up and down.

pattern 3

It takes 6 steps
to go up and down.

(a) How many steps would it take to go up and down the
8th pattern of stairs?

(b) How do you know?
Explain your method to your partner.

(c) How many steps would it take to go up and down the
10th pattern of stairs?

(d) How many steps would it take to go up and down the
100th pattern of stairs?

4 Look at these squares made on a pinboard.

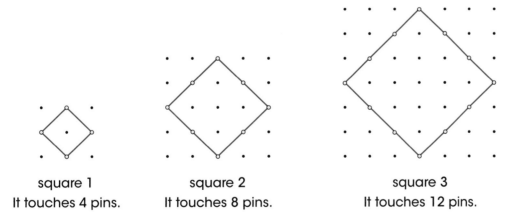

square 1
It touches 4 pins.

square 2
It touches 8 pins.

square 3
It touches 12 pins.

(a) How many pins should the 7th square touch?

(b) Explain to your partner how to work out the answer
without drawing a diagram.

What have you noticed in all these investigations?

What has your partner noticed?

Doubles

Let's investigate

What is the missing number?

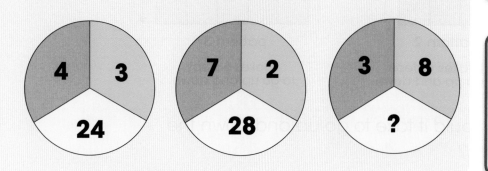

What rule connects 4, 3 and 24?

Does that rule work for 7, 2 and 28?

Use the rule to find the missing number.

1   Double these numbers.

   (a) 58   **(b)** 71   **(c)** 36   **(d)** 98

2   The rule for these number sequences is to double the previous number. What are the missing numbers?

   (a) 3, 6, 12, **?** , **?** , **?**

   (b) 5, 10, 20, **?** , **?** , **?**

3   Copy these tables. Use doubling to complete these table patterns.

Number	1	2	3	4	5	6	7	8	9	10
2×	2	4		8		12			18	20
4×			12					32	36	
8×					40		56		72	

Number	1	2	3	4	5	6	7	8	9	10
3×	3	6		12		18			27	30
6×			18					48	54	
12×					60		84		108	

4   Use doubling to complete this pattern:

   $1 \times 13 = 13$ $2 \times 13 = 26$ $4 \times 13 =$ **?** $8 \times 13 =$ **?**

5 Copy and complete the tables for these number machines.

Input	Output
4	
9	
18	
	32

Input	Output
5	
11	
45	
	17

6 Here are some triangle numbers.

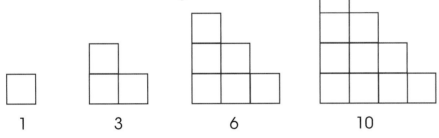

| 1 | 3 | 6 | 10 |

If you double a triangle number, you can make a rectangle.
Here, the fourth triangle number (10) has been doubled.

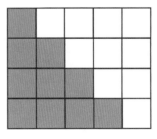

(a) What is special about the length and width of the rectangle?

(b) Double the other triangle numbers and then complete the sentence:

When I double a triangle number _____ .

7 A sequence starts 2, 3, 5, 9, 17...
Explain to your partner the rule for the sequence.

8 Find two examples to show that the following rule is true:
Any odd number is double a number and then add 1.

Multiplying

Let's investigate

The number in each square is the product of mutliplying together the two circles on either side. For example,

? × **?** = 14

Find the missing numbers.

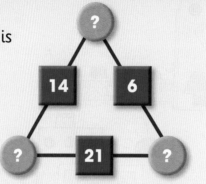

Vocabulary

grid method: a method of multiplication that uses a grid. For example, $27 \times 4 = 108$

	20	7
4	80	28

$80 + 28 = 108$

1 Use a number line to show how to calculate 23×4 using repeated addition.

+23

0   23

2 Abdul calculates 23×5 using partitioning.

$23 \times 5 = (20 \times 5) + (3 \times 5)$
$= 100 + 15$
$= 115$

Work out the value of these expressions using partitioning:

(a) 42×3

(b) 37×4

(c) 46×5

3 Estimate the value of these expressions. Then calculate the value.

(a) 47×5

(b) 29×4

(c) 89×3

(d) 74×4

4 Sultan uses the grid method to answer some calculations, but then spills ink on his work. What numbers are under the ink smudges?

(a) 47 × 3

×	40	7
3	⬛	21

⬛ + 21 = 141

(b) 93 × 4

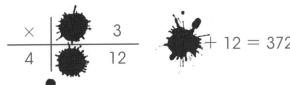

×	⬛	3
4	⬛	12

⬛ + 12 = 372

(c) 51 × 5

×	50	1
5	⬛	⬛

⬛ + ⬛ = 255

(d) 87 × 4

×	⬛	7
4	320	28

320 + 28 = 3⬛

5 Multiply together the numbers in the circles to calculate the products in the squares between them.
Copy the diagrams and fill in the missing numbers.

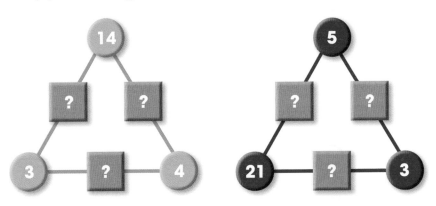

6 Pencils are sold in packs of five. Each pack costs 95 cents.
Fatima buys four packs of pencils.
How much does she spend?

5 pencils

7 Use the digits 2, 3 and 4 to make the expression with the greatest product.

? ? × ?

What is the product?

Measure

Measuring weight

Let's investigate

Each **cube** on the scales, weighs 5 kg.

How much does each **cone** weigh?

How much does each **sphere** weigh?

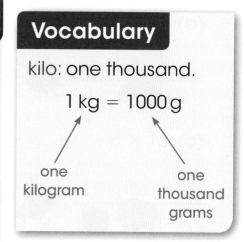

1   Read the scales to find out how much each package weighs.
    Write the letter for each package in order, from lightest to heaviest.

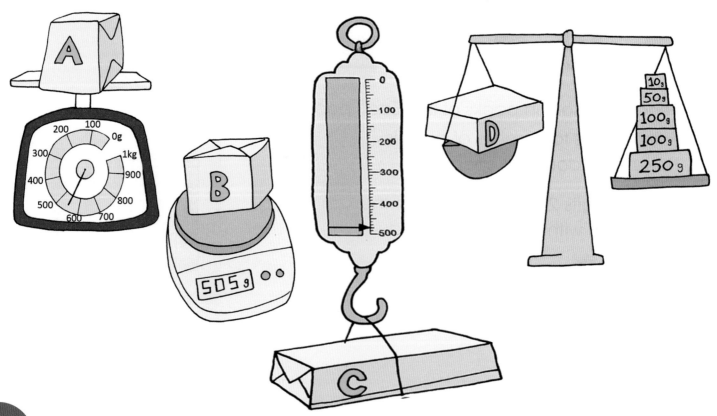

2

Kerry is going to make three different sorts of biscuit. These are the recipes:

Nut biscuits	Chocolate biscuits	Oat biscuits
Flour 225 g	Butter 100 g	Butter 175 g
Sugar 100 g	Sugar 50 g	Sugar 150 g
Butter 150 g	Flour 90 g	Oats 75 g
Nuts 50 g	Cocoa powder 15 g	Nuts 25 g

(a) What is the total weight of the ingredients for each recipe?

(b) How much of each of these ingredients are needed to make
all three recipes?

Flour ? g   Sugar ? g   Butter ? g   Nuts ? g

3 Hazel weighed one plastic cube. It weighed
4 grams. She put items from around the
classroom onto one side of some balance
scales. For each item, she counted how
many of her 4 g cubes were needed to
balance the scales.

(a) An eraser weighs 2 cubes.

(b) A mini stapler weighs 15 cubes.

(c) A pencil weighs 7 cubes.

(d) A sheet of paper weighs 1 cube.

How much did each item weigh in grams?

4 Saleem wants to make a set of weights by
putting cubes together. Each cube weighs 4 grams.
How many cubes does he need to use in
order to make:

(a) a 20 g weight?   (b) a 100 g weight?

(c) a 500 g weight?   (d) a 1 kg weight?

Telling the time (1)

Let's investigate

I looked at the clock reflected in the mirror when I left the house. I looked at the clock in the mirror again when I got home. What were the real times?

The time when I left the house

The time when I got home

Try looking at the pictures in a mirror.

1 On each of these clocks the minute hand is missing. With a partner, use the position of the hour hand to estimate where the minute hand should be. Then estimate the time.

The clock face has a scale of 1 to 12 for hours and a scale of 0 to 59 for minutes.

The minute hand would be pointing at about 30 minutes because the hour hand is half way between the numbers.

Estimate: 3:30

I estimate the time is half past three.

(a)

(b)

(c)
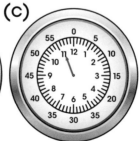

(d)
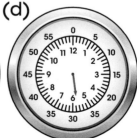

(e)
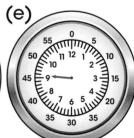

2 Write the time shown on the clocks below in digital time.

Here is an example.

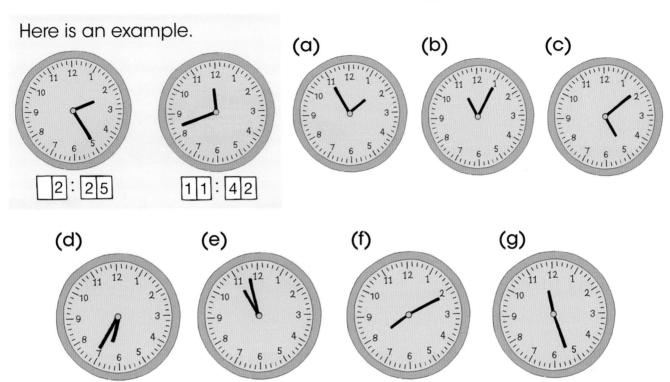

| 2 : 25 | | 11 : 42 |

3 Divide a piece of paper into two. Write
am in one space and **pm** in the other.

Draw three pictures in each part of the
page to show some things you do in
the 'am' and 'pm' of a typical day.

Look at Paolo's page as an example.
In the morning, Paolo puts
on his shoes to walk to school.
In the afternoon he plays football
with his friends after school.

Using timetables

Write a story that describes a journey between 4 places that takes 3 hours.

Example:
I started at **home**. I travelled by bus for **45 minutes** to **Riverton**. Then I walked for **1 hour and 30 minutes** to get to **Hillbury**. Then I took the train for **45 minutes** to get to **my friend's house**.

1   Use the timetable below to answer questions 1–3.

Train timetable			
	A	**B**	**C**
Ourtown	9:10 am	10:30 am	12:20 pm
Riverton	9:45 am	11:05 am	12:55 pm
Hillbury	10:15 am	11:35 am	1:25 pm
Newcity	11:30 am	12:50 pm	2:40 pm

For example, it takes 1 hour and 45 minutes to travel from Riverton to Newcity.

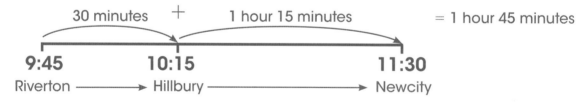

How long does it take for the train to travel:

(a) from Ourtown to Riverton?   **(b)** from Hillbury to Newcity?

(c) from Ourtown to Hillbury?   **(d)** from Ourtown to Newcity?

2 How long would I have to wait for a train if I arrived at:

(a) Ourtown station at 9:05 am?   (b) Riverton station at 10:45 am?

(c) Hillbury station at 11:15 am?   (d) Riverton station at 11:35 am?

3 Which is the latest train I can catch from Ourtown to arrive at:

(a) Riverton station by 10:00 am?   (b) Hillbury station by 2:15 pm?

(c) Newcity station by 1:30 pm?   (d) Hillbury station by 1:20 pm?

4 These timetables have been torn! Fill in the gaps.

Bus timetable				
Hospital	8:25 am	11:45 am	1:30 pm	4:35 pm
Shopping centre	8:55 am	12:15 pm	2:00 pm	(a)
Industrial area	9:40 am	1:00 pm	(b)	(c)
Railway station	10:45 am	2:05 pm	(d)	(e)

Bus timetable				
Railways station	10:50 am	2:10 pm	(f)	(g)
Industrial area	11:55 am	3:15 pm	(h)	(i)
Shopping centre	12:40 pm	4:00 pm	5:45 pm	(j)
Hospital	1:10 pm	4:30 pm	6:15 pm	9:20 pm

5 Look at the map. What route might a bus take through the town?

Write a timetable for the bus's route. Start at the Bus Station.

Area (1)

area: the size of a surface measured in square units.

fraction: part of a shape or number.

Let's investigate

Maria laid square carpet tiles on her floor. On the first day she only laid one tile, on the second day she laid two carpet tiles and on the third day she laid three carpet tiles. Each day she laid one more tile than the day before.

What area of floor had she covered at the end of 10 days, in squares?

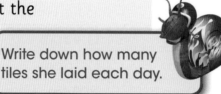

Write down how many tiles she laid each day.

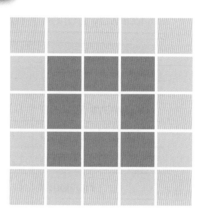

1 This pattern is made from 1 cm square tiles.

(a) What is the total area covered by the pattern in squares?

(b) What is the total area covered by the pattern in square centimetres?

(c) What area of the pattern is red in square centimetres?

(d) What area of the pattern is orange in square centimetres?

(e) What area of the pattern is green in square centimetres?

Make your own pattern on a grid of centimetre squares like this.

Use three colours.

Write down the area of each colour.

What fraction of the pattern is made up of each colour?

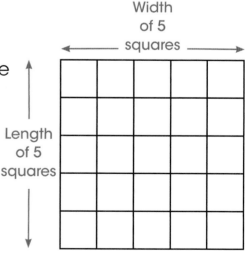

Width of 5 squares

Length of 5 squares

2 Count the squares below to find the area of the **whole** rectangle, the area of the **shaded part**, and the area of the **not shaded** part. Record what fraction of the rectangle area is shaded.

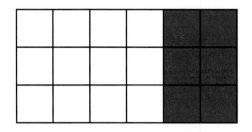

Rectangle 1

Area of the whole rectangle = **?** squares.

Area shaded = **?** squares.

Area not shaded = **?** squares.

Fraction of the rectangle shaded = **?** squares.

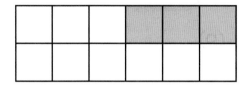

Rectangle 2

Area of the whole rectangle = **?** squares.

Area shaded = **?** squares.

Area not shaded = **?** squares.

Fraction of the rectangle shaded = **?** squares.

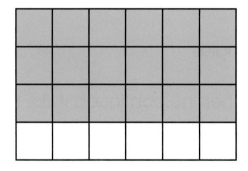

Rectangle 3

Area of the whole rectangle = **?** squares.

Area shaded = **?** squares.

Area not shaded = **?** squares.

Fraction of the rectangle shaded = **?** squares.

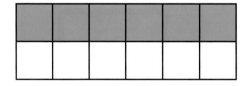

Rectangle 4

Area of the whole rectangle = **?** squares.

Area shaded = **?** squares.

Area not shaded = **?** squares.

Fraction of the rectangle shaded = **?** squares.

Perimeter (1)

Let's investigate

A rectangle has a perimeter of 14 cm.
What could be the length of each of its sides?
Find all the possible answers using only whole cm.

perimeter: the distance around a shape.

?
? ?
?

Remember that the opposite sides of a rectangle are the same length.

1   Class 4 have made some straw shapes with a perimeter of 24 cm. In each picture one of the labels has fallen off. Work out the length that should be on the missing label.

(a)
2 cm
5 cm
8 cm
6 cm
?

(b)
5 cm
4 cm
7 cm
?

(c)
1 cm
?
7 cm
6 cm
3 cm
2 cm

2   Ali is making a pattern of different sized rectangles with different coloured string.
The pattern started like this:

Then he continued it like this:

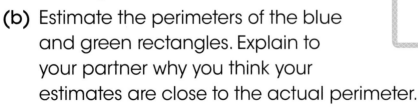

3 cm
2 cm   2 cm
3 cm

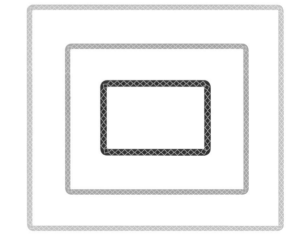

(a) What is the perimeter of the red rectangle?

(b) Estimate the perimeters of the blue and green rectangles. Explain to your partner why you think your estimates are close to the actual perimeter.

3 **(a)** Cut a piece of string or thread so that it measures 24 cm.
Stick it carefully onto squared paper to make a rectangle
and label the length of each side.

(b) Try making different rectangles with other pieces of 24 cm
string or thread.

4 Halima says that because her table is a square,
she can work out the perimeter of the top of
the table by just measuring one side.

Is she correct? Explain why.

The perimeter of
the table top is
4 metres.

Remember that a
square has 4 sides that
are all the **same** length.

5 Each of the shapes below was made using four of these squares.

5 cm

5 cm

Work out the perimeter of each shape.

(a)

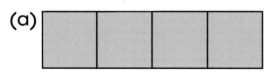

Don't count the lines
inside the shape; the
perimeter is only the
length around the
outside of a shape.

(b)   **(c)**

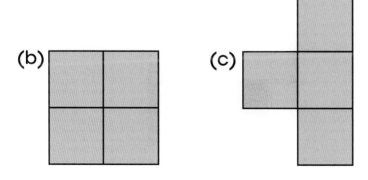

Handling data

Tally charts and bar charts

Let's investigate

Anya and Gisele have collected data about the sports their classmates like to watch. But they forgot to write in the labels.

Sport	Number of people
(a)	卌 ||||
(b)	卌 卌 卌 ||
(c)	卌 |
(d)	|||

Copy their chart, and use the clues below to complete it.

- The least popular sport was **hockey**.
- **Football** was more popular than **motor racing**.
- 9 people chose **tennis**.

Vocabulary

data: information collected by counting or measuring.

table: a way of showing data in rows and columns.

tally chart: a chart that uses marks to record counting. For example,

	Tally
Buses (B)	||||
Cars (C)	卌 ||||
Vans (V)	卌

bar chart: a graph with bars to show how large a quantity or number is.

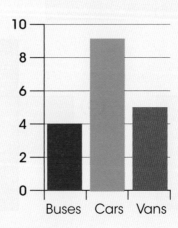

1 Five children have made a statement about how many badges they have collected.

A
I collected more badges than Sarah.

B
I did not collect the most badges.

C
Leroy and I collected 35 badges altogether.

D
I collected 2 badges less than Janice.

E
I collected more badges than Florine.

Use the bar chart to work out which child said each statement. Work with a partner.

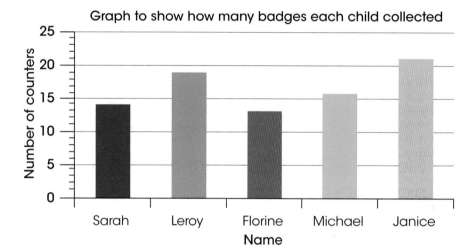

Graph to show how many badges each child collected

Number of counters (y-axis: 0, 5, 10, 15, 20, 25)

Name (x-axis: Sarah, Leroy, Florine, Michael, Janice)

2 Class 4 collected data about the traffic passing their school in 1 hour. Make a bar chart from the data in the tally chart opposite. Decide on a scale and explain why you have chosen that scale.

Type of transport	Number seen (tally)
car	‖‖‖ ‖‖‖ ‖‖‖ ‖‖‖ ‖‖‖ ‖‖‖ ‖‖‖
bicycle	‖‖‖ ‖‖
motorcycle	‖‖‖ ‖‖‖‖
van	‖‖‖ ‖‖‖ ‖‖‖ ‖
bus	‖‖‖ ‖
lorry	‖‖‖

Use your bar chart to decide if these statements are true or false.

(a) More cars passed the school than any other vehicle.

(b) 6 more vans were seen than motorcycles.

(c) More than 15 of the vehicles had only 2 wheels.

(d) There were 30 fewer lorries than cars.

(e) 77 vehicles passed the school.

Pictograms

Let's investigate

The key has been torn off the pictogram below.

Sweet colour	Number in the packet
red	🐟 🐟 🐟
yellow	🐟 ◗
green	🐟 🐟 ◗

How many sweets might each picture represent?

Explain your answer.

What fraction sweet is here? How many sweets does it represent? There is more than one correct answer!

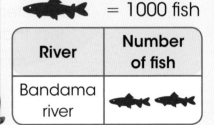
1 Class 8 are in a different school to class 4. They created this pictogram of the traffic passing their school in 1 hour.

Type of transport	Number of vehicles
car	⚙️⚙️ ⚙️⚙️ ⚙️⚙️ ⚙️⚙️ ⚙️◗
bicycle	⚙️⚙️
motorcycle	⚙️⚙️ ⚙️◗
van	⚙️⚙️ ⚙️
bus	◗
lorry	◗

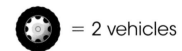 = 2 vehicles

Use the pictogram to answer these questions:

(a) How many vehicles with two wheels passed the school?

(b) How many more cars passed the school than vans?

(c) How many fewer bicycles passed the school than motorcycles?

(d) How many vehicles passed the school altogether?

2 Compare Class 8's pictogram from question 1 with Class 4's tally chart below.

Type of transport	Number seen (tally)
car	⊥⊥⊥ ⊥⊥⊥ ⊥⊥⊥ ⊥⊥⊥ ⊥⊥⊥ ⊥⊥⊥ |||
bicycle	⊥⊥⊥ ||
motorcycle	⊥⊥⊥ ||||
van	⊥⊥⊥ ⊥⊥⊥ ⊥⊥⊥	
bus	⊥⊥⊥	
lorry	|||

(a) How many more vehicles passed Class 8's school than Class 4's school?

(b) What is the difference between the number of vans passing each school?

(c) With a partner write three sentences describing how the traffic at the two schools is similar and three sentences describing how the traffic is different.

3 The votes are in for the musical talent competition.
This pictogram shows the votes that were received for each music act.

🎵 = 10 votes

			🎵	
		🎵	🎵	
		🎵	🎵	🎵
🎵	🎵	🎵	🎵	🎵
🎵	🎵	🎵	🎵	🎵
Act 1	Act 2	Act 3	Act 4	Act 5

(a) Estimate how many votes were received each by Act 1 and Act 5.

(b) What is the difference in the number of votes given to the highest- and lowest-scoring acts?

(c) About how many votes were received altogether?

(d) Acts 1, 3 and 4 go through to the next round. The table of the results is shown opposite.

Draw a pictogram to show the results.

Act	Votes
1	45
3	42
4	58

What scale will you use? Don't forget to add a key!

Carroll diagrams (1)

Let's investigate

Conrad made this Carroll diagram.

	even	not even
multiple of 10		
not a multiple of 10		

I can find a number to fit in every section of my Carroll diagram.

Is Conrad correct?
Explain how you know.

'Conrad is correct/incorrect because ...'

Vocabulary

sort/classify: to group things according to particular features.

Carroll diagram: a way of sorting things into those that have a particular feature and those that do not. For example,

	'this'	not 'this'
'that'		
not 'that'		

Carroll diagrams are named after Lewis Carroll who wrote 'Alice's adventures in Wonderland'.

1 Sylvester has decided to sort his shopping onto his shelves with a Carroll diagram.

   (a) What labels could be on the columns and rows?

   (b) Draw the Carroll diagram and add the labels. Add one more item to each shelf that matches the labels.

   (c) Sort the items below into a different Carroll diagram. What labels does your diagram have?

2   Class 4 drew pictures of some of the vehicles passing their school.
    The pictures have been arranged into this Carroll diagram.

(a) How many vehicles are in the correct sections of the Carroll diagram?

(b) Copy the Carroll diagram below. Complete it using the same pictures
    that are in the Carroll diagram above.

	bicycle	not bicycle
red	?	?
not red	?	?

Venn diagrams

Vocabulary

Venn diagram: a way of sorting things according to different features. For example,

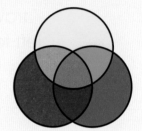

Venn diagrams are named after John Venn, a British mathematician.

Let's investigate

16 children in the class like apples.

11 children in the class like bananas.

7 children in the class both like apples and bananas.

3 children in the class do not like any fruit.

How many children are there in the class?

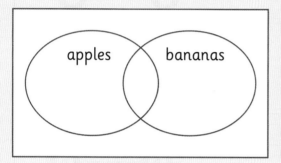

Draw your own Venn diagram and fill in the gaps. Check that your Venn diagram matches each statement above.

1   Look at the children below.

Copy the Venn diagram and sort each child into the correct section.

2   Draw the Venn diagram and look at each section.

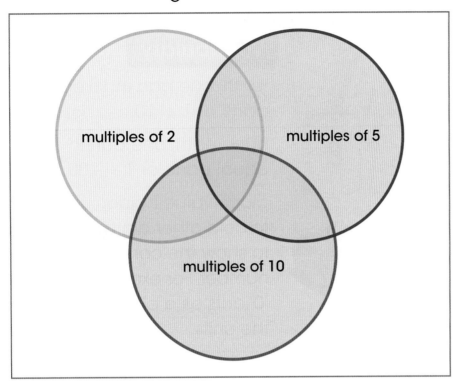

Think of numbers that could go in each section.
Is there a section that cannot have any numbers?
Explain your reasoning to your partner or group.

Mark a small ✗ on your diagram where you think there may not be any possible numbers.

3   Place the whole numbers from 1 to 30 in the correct section of your Venn diagram from question 2.

4   Place the numbers below in the correct part of your Venn diagram. Explain your reasoning to your partner or group.

| 100 | 188 | 235 | 487 | 650 | 712 | 823 | 945 |

Choose 5 more numbers to place in your Venn diagram.

Look at your completed Venn diagram. Did you correctly guess which section would not have any numbers?
Discuss what you have found out with your partner or group.

Number

Money

Let's investigate

Freya has these cards.

Use **all** the cards to make as many amounts of money as possible less than $9.

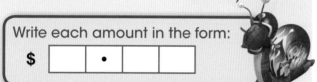

Write each amount in the form:

$ [ ] • [ ] [ ]

Order the amounts from smallest to largest.

Round each amount to the nearest dollar.

Vocabulary

tenth: one part in 10 equal parts, or $1 \div 10$.

hundredth: one part in 100 equal parts, or $1 \div 100$.

place value holder: use of zero to hold other digits in position to show the correct size of a number. For example, in 0.4 the '0' acts as a placeholder for the units.

T	U	•	tenths	hundredths
	0	•	4	

1 The orange numbers on the place value charts below represent amounts of money in dollars.

Write each amount in **figures** and then **words**.

(a)

10	20	30	40	50	60	70	80	90
1	2	3	4	5	6	7	8	9
0.1	0.2	0.3	0.4	0.5	0.6	0.7	0.8	0.9
0.01	0.02	0.03	0.04	0.05	0.06	0.07	0.08	0.09

(b)

10	20	30	40	50	60	70	80	90
1	2	3	4	5	6	7	8	9
0.1	0.2	0.3	0.4	0.5	0.6	0.7	0.8	0.9
0.01	0.02	0.03	0.04	0.05	0.06	0.07	0.08	0.09

(c)

100	200	300	400	500	600	700	800	900
10	20	30	40	50	60	70	80	90
1	2	3	4	5	6	7	8	9
0.1	0.2	0.3	0.4	0.5	0.6	0.7	0.8	0.9
0.01	0.02	0.03	0.04	0.05	0.06	0.07	0.08	0.09

2 Write the following amounts of money in figures. Use a grid like this one.

$ | | | • | | |

(a) twenty-six dollars and seventy cents
(b) ten dollars and fifteen cents
(c) forty dollars and five cents
(d) thirteen dollars and seven cents

3 Order the following amounts of money from the smallest amount to the largest amount.
(a) $74.09 $47.99 $97.49 $79.94
(b) $46.64 $64.46 $64.64 $46.46
(c) $45.05 $54.54 $45.45 $54.05 $45.54

4 Round these amounts to the nearest dollar.
(a) $45.09   (b) 45.54   (c) $45.45

5 Fatima and Ailsa have the following coins.
They share the money out fairly.
Which coins could each girl have?

Coin	Number of coins
5 cents	4
10 cents	1
25 cents	2
50 cents	1

6 Order the following amounts of money from the smallest amount to the largest amount.

First write all the amounts in the same format.

(a) 34 dollars   3 dollars and 50 cents $33.03 $34.50 $33.30
(b) 300 cents   30 dollars   334 cents $34.30 $3.30
(c) 94 cents   490 cents $4.09 $0.49   4 dollars and 99 cents

7 The cost of my shopping is $5.00 when rounded to the nearest dollar.
(a) What is the greatest amount I could have spent?
(b) What is the smallest amount I could have spent?
Explain to your partner how you decided.

Positive and negative numbers

Let's investigate

Find out about creatures that live below sea level.

How deep do they live?

sea level

1 Look at this thermometer.

Which numbers are represented by the boxes marked **A**, **B** and **C**?

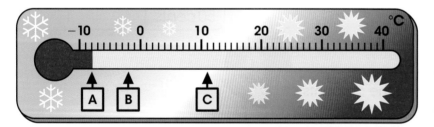

2 Which temperature is the coldest?

−6 °C   0 °C   1 °C   −2 °C

3 The temperature in a town was 5 °C.

The temperature dropped by 9 degrees C overnight.

What was the lowest night-time temperature?

Vocabulary

positive number: a number greater than zero. For example, 5 or 32.

negative number: a number less than zero. For example, −1 or −9.

°C or degrees C: a way of measuring temperature, to say how hot or cold something is, or a change in temperature. For example,

'It is 18 °C today' or 'The temperature has gone down by 5 degrees C'.

'C' is short for Celsius, named after Anders Celsius, a Swedish astronomer.

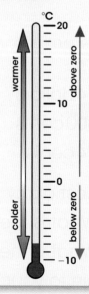

4   Use the number line to help you work out the answers
    to the questions.

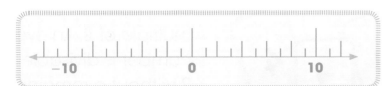

(a) What temperature is 6 degrees warmer than −4 °C?
(b) What temperature is 5 degrees colder than 1 °C?
(c) What temperature is 3 degrees warmer than −2 °C?
(d) What temperature is 3 degrees higher than 0 °C?
(e) What temperature is 5 degrees higher than −1 °C?

5   Use the signs < or > to make these statements correct.
(a) −1 ? −5
(b) −3 ? −6
(c) −5 ? 4
(d) −2 ? −12

6   The numbers on the number line below represent letters of the alphabet.

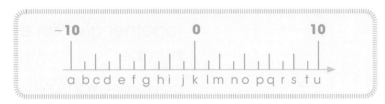

Copy and complete the table to solve the code and find out
where emperor penguins live.

−10	3	9	−10	7	−8	9	−2	−8	−10

Odd and even numbers

Let's investigate

Jiao has these cards.

My number has three digits. It is an even number.

What numbers might be Jiao's?

Think about the units digit.

1   Write all the odd numbers greater than 20 and less than 30.

2   Write an even number to make this statement true. $12 < \boxed{?} < 16$

3   Here are three number cards.

Use each card **once** to make the answer to each calculation below an even number.

$\boxed{?} \times 2 =$

$10 \div \boxed{?} =$

$14 - \boxed{?} =$

4   Choose three of these number cards to make an even number greater than 500.

5   Solve these number problems.

    (a) I am a two-digit number less than 20.
        I am odd.
        The sum of my digits is 10.
        Which number am I?

    (b) I am a two-digit number.
        I am an even number.
        I am greater than 3×7.
        I am less than 4×6.
        Which number am I?

    (c) I am a two-digit number less than 80.
        I am even.
        My digits are the same.
        I am a multiple of 4.
        Which number am I?

6   Draw the Venn diagram below.

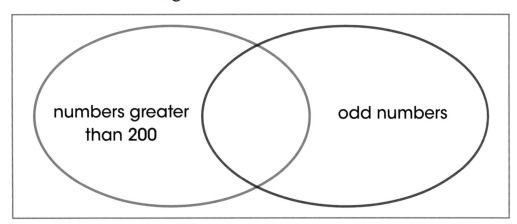

    Write these numbers in the correct section.
    57   309   450

7   Martha says, 'I added three odd numbers and my answer was 30'.
    Explain why Martha cannot be correct.

8   Ahmed says, 'I add two odd numbers together and my answer is odd'.
    Give a counter-example to show that Ahmed is wrong.

Adding and subtracting near multiples of 10

Let's investigate

Imagine you are in a number maze.

Start in any of the blue spaces.

Move through the maze adding each number in your path. Do **not** go into the same space more than once.

How can you reach the finish with a total of 30?

Look for pairs of numbers that add up to 10. Look for groups of three numbers that add up to 10.

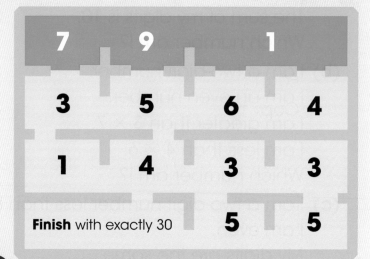

Finish with exactly 30

1   Imagine you throw three hoops over these cones.
    Add together the number of each cone you get a hoop on.
    You have three throws a turn.
    What different totals can you make on each turn?

30   90   40

2   Each crown has three jewels. The total value of the jewels on each crown is $1000. Work out the missing values.

(a)
500 400 ?

(b)
150 ? 600

(c)
? 350 350

(d)
250 ? 550

(e)
850 ? 100

(f)
450 ? 300

3

(a) Sam, Tim, Amy, Ian and Ria are shopping.
Each person buys two items of clothing.

Copy the table below.

Then choose two items for each person to buy
and work out how much they need to pay.

You could use a
multiple of 10 and
compensate.

Name	Clothing item 1	Clothing item 2	Total price
Sam			
Tim			
Amy			
Ian			
Ria			

(b) When they get to the till they find out that there is a discount
on some of the items. Each person needs to subtract their
discount from their total price.

Copy the table below. What is the final price each person pays?

Name	Discount	Final price
Sam	$19	
Tim	$11	
Amy	$31	
Ian	$22	
Ria	$28	

4

Number sentence stories

Look at Sam's number story. Write a shopping
story for the number sentence below:

$68 - 56 + 23 = 35$

I had $45 and I spent
$20 on a game and $9
on food. I had $16 left.
I can write that as
$45 - 20 - 9 = 16$

Choosing the best method

Let's investigate

Make the number sentence below true.
You can use each digit from 1 to 9 only **once**.

$$? \; ? \; ? + ? \; ? \; ? + ? \; ? \; ? = 999$$

There is more than one solution.

> To get the last 9 in 999, the units digits in the other numbers must add up to a number ending in 9.

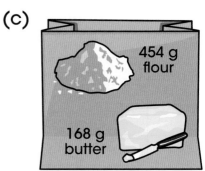

1   Work out the total weight in each shopping bag.

(a)
225 g cheese
480 g oranges

(b)
678 g potatoes
303 g tomatoes

(c)
454 g flour
168 g butter

(d)
349 g beans
482 g rice

(e)
498 g apples
502 g carrots

2   George takes the following amounts of ingredients out of the shopping bags.

How much does each bag weigh now?

(a) 186 g cheese   (b) 122 g tomatoes   (c) 355 g flour

(d) 428 g rice   (e) 243 g apples.

3 Look at these problems.

238 + 447	702 − 695	312 − 21	125 + 112
432 − 179	581 + 307	786 + 926	522 − 349
603 + 497	595 − 403	782 − 779	638 + 843

Decide whether you will use a mental method or a written method to solve each one. Make a table like this one.

Mental method		Written method	
Problem	**Solution**	**Problem**	**Solution**
Example: $162 - 11 =$ −1 −10 **151 152 162**	151	Example: $362 - 138$ $362 = 300 + 50 + 12$ $138 = 100 + 30 + 8$ $300 - 100 = 200$ $50 - 30 = 20$ $12 - 8 = 4$ $200 + 20 + 4 = 224$	224

Write the problem in the part of the table that shows which method you have chosen. Then solve the problem.

Explain to your partner or group why you used your chosen method.

If you think there is a better method that your partner could have used, tell them why.

More multiplication

Let's investigate

Here are four cards.

Place the cards in a square and multiply across the rows.

 $4 \times 3 = 12$

 $6 \times 5 = 30$

The product of 4 and 3 is 12. The product is the answer to the multiplication.

Move the cards and multiply again.

 $3 \times 4 = 12$

 $5 \times 6 = 30$

So far we have found only two **different** products.

Move the cards and multiply again.

How many **different** products can you find?

1   Copy and complete these multiplication triangles.
    The product of the two circles on each line is the number in the square.

(a)
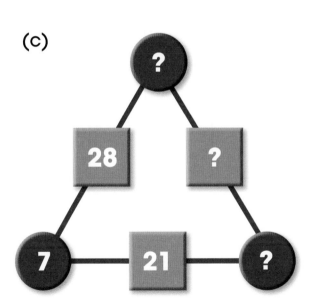

(b)
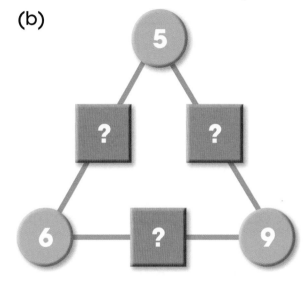

(c)
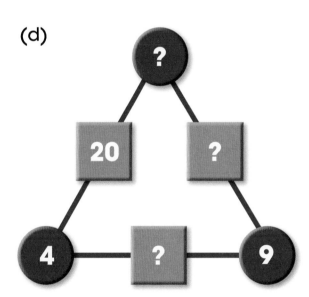

(d)

2   Complete these calculations.
    (a) 78 × 6
    (b) 43 × 9
    (c) 29 × 9
    (d) 37 × 6

3 This is a multiplication grid.

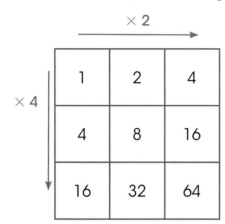

Copy and complete these multiplication grids.

(a)

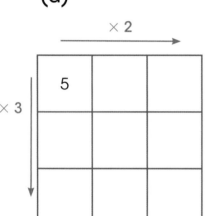

(b) **(c)**

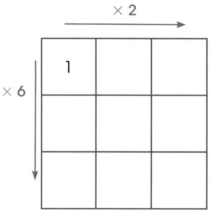

4 Use the numbers 3, 6 and 18 to complete these calculations.

(a) ? × ? = ?

(b) ? ÷ ? = ?

(c) ? × ? = ?

(d) ? ÷ ? = ?

5 David uses the known fact $6 \times 7 = 42$, to help him calculate 6×14. The table shows some known facts and some calculations.

	Known fact	Calculation
(a)	$34 \times 5 = 170$	$34 \times 6 =$ **?**
(b)	$48 \times 4 = 192$	$48 \times 8 =$ **?**
(c)	$54 \times 6 = 324$	$54 \times 3 =$ **?**
(d)	$23 \times 6 = 138$	$23 \times 7 =$ **?**

I know that $6 \times 7 = 42$, and I know that 14 is double 7. So, if I double 42 then I can find out the answer to 6×14. The answer is 84.

Work with a partner. Explain how you would work out the answers to each calculation starting from the known fact.

6 **Discuss** with your partner the most efficient way to work out the following calculations.

Then work out the correct answer and choose a different method to check your answer is correct.

(a) 78×8

(b) 66×5

(c) 76×5

(d) 21×9

Division

Let's investigate

Each of these numbers gives a remainder of 1 when it is divided by 4:

17   81   49

Find numbers that have a remainder of 2 when they are divided by 4.

What do you notice about the numbers?

> Write the numbers in order and look at the pattern of the units digits. What do you notice?

Here is an example of rounding up.
A minibus holds 12 people.
How many minibuses do we need for 28 people?

28 ÷ 12 = 2 remainder 4

> You need to round up to 3 so that everyone has a seat.

We need 3 minibuses.

1   Copy and complete this remainder chart for 24.
    The first one has been done for you.

24 divided by	2	3	4	5	6	7	8	9	10
Remainder	0	?	?	?	?	?	?	?	?

Describe your results.

2   Darina divided 72 by 4 using the method of halving and then halving again.

72 ÷ 4 = 18

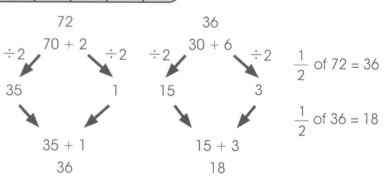

Use this method to calculate:

(a) 76 ÷ 4   (b) 68 ÷ 4

3 Pablo divided 72 by 4 using a number line.

8 lots of 4   10 lots of 4

0   32   72 $72 \div 4 = 18$

Use this method to calculate:

(a) $95 \div 5$ **(b)** $54 \div 3$

4 Kimi used repeated subtraction
to calculate $72 \div 4$.

```
72
40    4 × 10
32
32    4 × 8
 0              72 ÷ 4 = 18
```

Use this method to calculate:

(a) $75 \div 5$ **(b)** $48 \div 3$

5 Complete these calculations using the most efficient method.

(a) $98 \div 7$ **(b)** $64 \div 9$ **(c)** $74 \div 8$ **(d)** $84 \div 6$

6 Copy and complete
these division wheels.

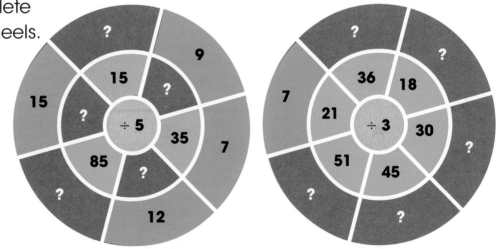

7 **(a)** Stamps are sold in books of six. Peng needs stamps to post 37 letters.
How many books of stamps does he need?

(b) Ebere has 87 flowers. She puts 10 flowers in each bunch.
How many bunches can she make?

(c) There are 27 students in a class. Six students sit at each table.
How many tables are needed?

Geometry

Angles and turning

Let's investigate

2D shapes with 4 sides are called quadrilaterals. This quadrilateral has no right angles.

Draw a quadrilateral with 1 right angle. Can you draw quadrilaterals with 2, 3 or 4 right angles?

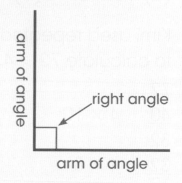

1   Here are four angles, A, B, C and D. Put them in order of size starting with the smallest.

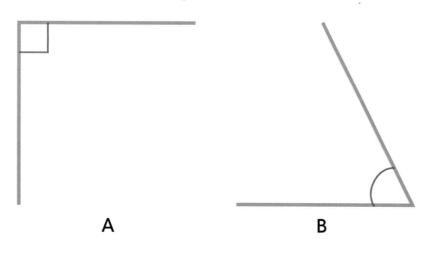

A

B

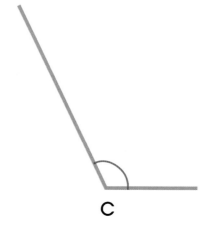

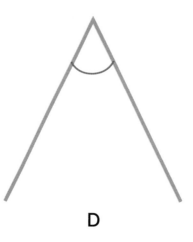

C

D

2 Look at these shapes. How many right angles does each shape have?

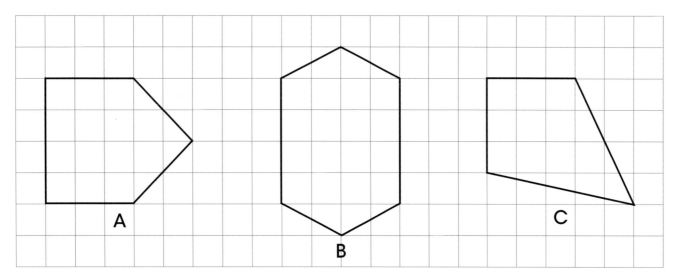

3 Cut out a square piece of paper. Fold it in half along a diagonal. You now have a triangle with a 90° angle and two angles of 45°.

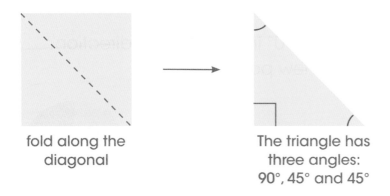

fold along the diagonal

The triangle has three angles: 90°, 45° and 45°

Use your triangle to help you estimate the size of these angles.

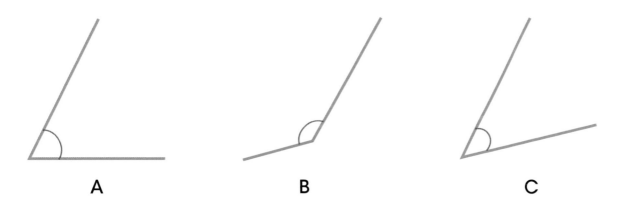

A   B   C

4   Here are five angle cards.

Put the cards in order of size
starting with the smallest angle.

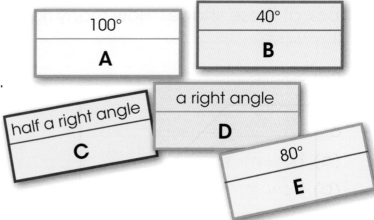

5   Here is a spinner.

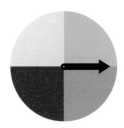

The arrow on the spinner turns through 90° in a clockwise direction.
(a) Which drawing below shows the new position?

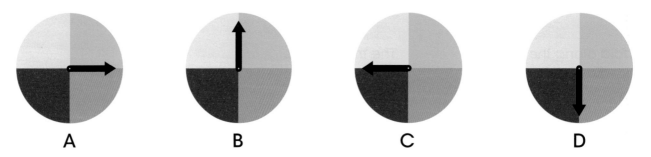

(b) The arrow spins through a whole turn.
    How many degrees does it turn through?

6 This shape is three-quarters of a circle.
It is drawn on the ground.

Roz stands at the centre and faces along
one straight edge. She turns to face along the
other straight edge.

   (a) How many right angles does she turn through?

   (b) How many degrees does she turn through?

7 Work with a partner. Look at the pattern together.
See how many different right-angled shapes you can find.

Use the measuring device you made for question 3 to help
you identify the right angles.

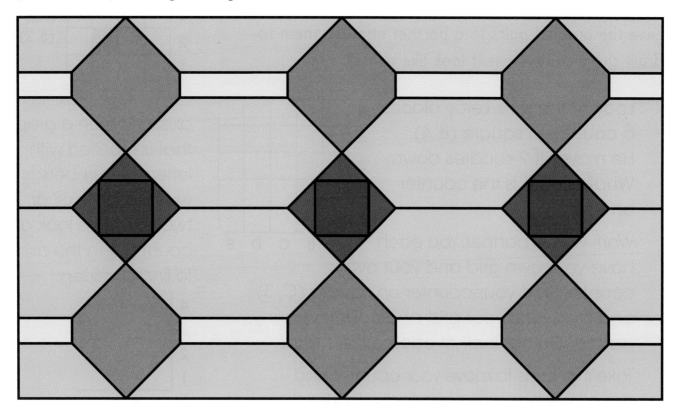

Position and direction

Let's investigate

Copy the grid. Don't forget to label the axes! Shade in squares for the following ordered pairs:

(B, 3) (C, 3) (D, 3)

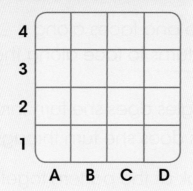

What is the name of the shape you have made?

Draw a picture on a grid.

Write a set of ordered pairs to make the picture.

Give the ordered pairs to a partner and ask them to draw the picture. Does it look like yours?

1 Look at the grid. Leroy places a counter in square (B, 4). He moves it 2 squares down. What square is the counter on now?

Work with a partner. You each have your own grid and your own counter. Start your counter on square (C, 3) and then hide your grid and counter from your partner. Do not look at each other's grids.

Take it in turns to move your counter and describe where you have moved it. Use the words 'up', 'down', 'left' and 'right' when describing how many squares your counter has moved.

Your partner has to move their counter by following your instructions. Check that your partner's counter is now in the same place as your counter.

ordered pair: a pair of letters or numbers that show a position on a grid.

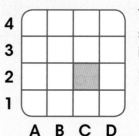

The square is at (C, 2).

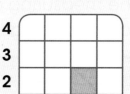

The square is at (3, 2).

axis: a line on a graph that is labelled with letters or numbers; we say one 'axis' or two 'axes'. We look or count along the axis to find a value.

2   Draw a grid with 6 by 6 squares.
    Plot the route described below.

    Start at the dot so that you are facing in the direction of the arrow.
    Now move:

    - Forward 4 squares.
    - Turn right through 1 right angle.
    - Forward 2 squares.
    - Turn right through 2 right angles.
    - Forward 2 squares.
    - Turn left through 1 right angle.
    - Forward 2 squares.
    - Turn left through 1 right angle.
    - Forward 1 square.
    - Stop.

    What capital letter have you drawn?

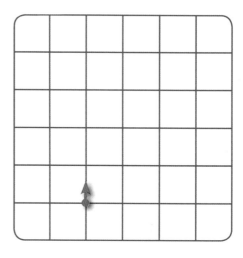

3   (a) Draw a grid with 6 by 6 squares.
         Label the axes like those opposite.

    (b) Shade the following squares on your grid:
         (2, 3)   (2, 4)   (2, 5)
         (3, 4)   (3, 5)   (4, 4)
         (4, 5)   (5, 4)   (5, 5)

    (c) What is the name of the shape you
         have made?

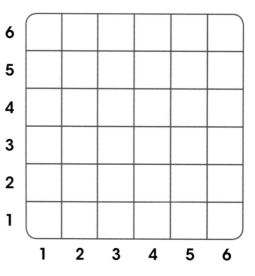

4   Look at the letter F drawn on the grid.
    Write down the position of each square
    that is shaded.

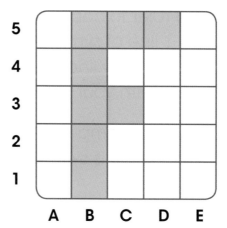

Symmetry

Let's investigate

You have four identical squares.

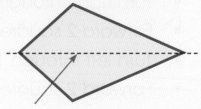

How many ways can you arrange them edge to edge to make a symmetrical shape?

Record your results.

Now try using five squares.

> Use cut-out shapes to experiment. Record your results on squared paper. Remember to mark the line of symmetry.

1   Copy this grid and the shaded shape.
    Shade one more square so that the shape has 1 line of symmetry.

    Draw the line of symmetry on your diagram and label it.

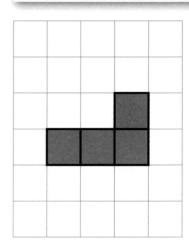

2   This is a shape made from four regular triangles.

    Use a ruler to copy the shape.
    Draw 1 line of symmetry on the shape.
    Is this the only line of symmetry?
    Discuss with your partner.

3   Copy and complete the diagram to make a shape that is symmetrical about the mirror line.

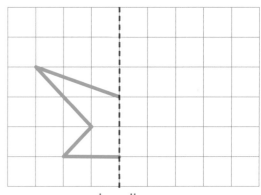

mirror line

4 Find all the different shapes in this pattern.

 Here is an example:

square

Draw each shape.

5 A sheet of paper is folded once.
A shape is cut out as shown.
Describe the shape that is cut out.
How many lines of symmetry does it have?

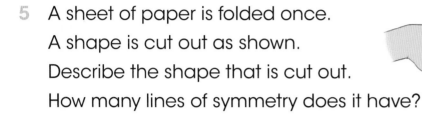

cut →

6 The capital letter E has one line of symmetry.

Write down all the capital letters that have lines of symmetry.
Some capital letters have more than one line of symmetry.
Can you find some examples?

7 Explore how you can cut a square shape
from a piece of paper that is folded once.

There is more than
one way of doing this.

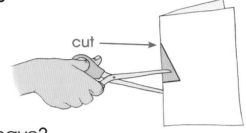

8 Look at this pattern.
It is made up of different shapes.
Find some symmetrical shapes in
the pattern. Here is an example:

line of
symmetry
(mirror line)

2D shapes

Let's investigate

Two identical right-angled triangles are made by cutting a rectangle in half.

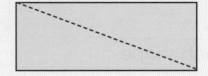

The triangles are joined together, edge to edge, to make a new shape.

Here is one possible shape.

What other shapes can you make by joining the triangles together?

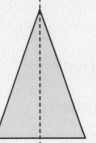

> Copy and cut out the triangles, then rearrange them. See how many different shapes you can make.

Vocabulary

polygon: a 2D shape with 3 or more straight sides and angles.

quadrilateral: a 4-sided polygon.

parallelogram: a quadrilateral with opposite lengths that are parallel to each other; opposite sides are equal in length and there are no right angles.

heptagon: a 7-sided polygon.

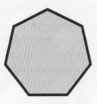

regular polygon: polygon with sides of equal length and angles of equal size.

parallel: two lines that are the same distance apart all along their length; the two lines will never cross.

octagon: an 8-sided polygon.

1   Here are seven shapes.

(a) How many of the shapes are heptagons?

(b) Which shapes are hexagons?

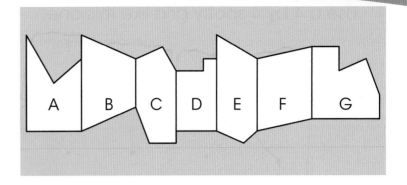

2   Name these quadrilaterals:

(a) It has 4 right angles. The sides are not all the same length.

(b) It has two pairs of opposite sides that are equal in length. No angle is a right angle.

(c) It has 4 lines of symmetry. The angles are all right angles.

3   Here are six shapes labelled A to F.

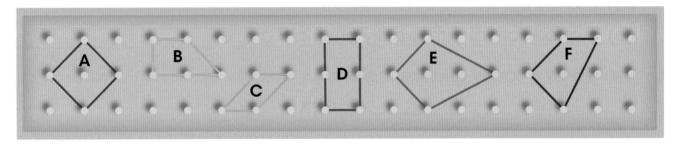

Copy the table and enter the letters to show the properties of each shape.

	only 1 pair of equal sides	2 pairs of equal sides	4 equal sides
Has at least 1 right angle			
Has no right angles			

4 Use a 4 by 4 spotty grid like this one.

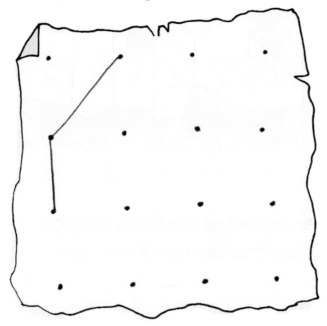

Join dots to make the following shapes:

(a) a hexagon with at least one right angle.

(b) a quadrilateral with exactly one right angle.

5 Use a 6 by 6 spotty grid like this one.

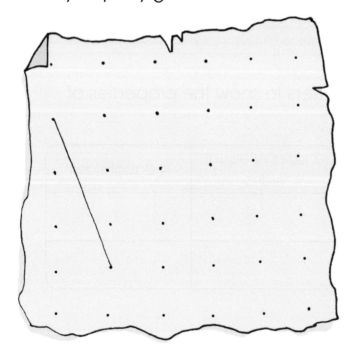

Draw the line shown.
Draw three more lines to make a square.

6   What shape is Lucas thinking of?

My shape has 4 right angles. It has 4 sides. The shape is regular.

7   Here is a pattern made of two different shapes.
One shape is a square.
What is the name of the other shape?

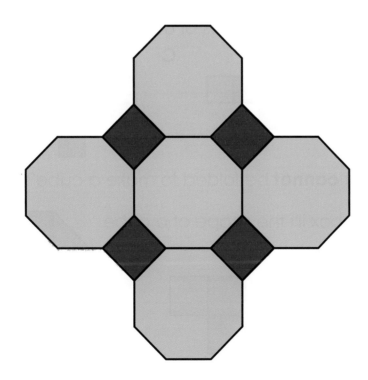

3D shapes

Let's investigate

Imagine you have two identical cubes.

Place them together so that a face on one cube is against a face on the other cube.

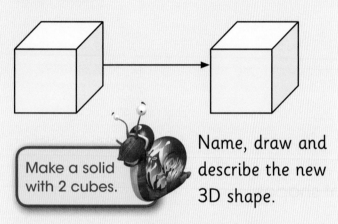

Make a solid with 2 cubes.

Name, draw and describe the new 3D shape.

How many faces, edges and vertices does it have?

tetrahedron: a 3D shape with 4 triangular faces.

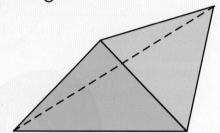

net: a 2D diagram that can be folded to make a 3D shape with no gaps or overlap.

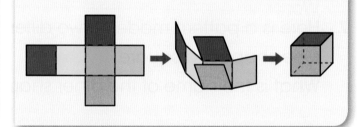

1   Here are four different arrangements of 6 squares.

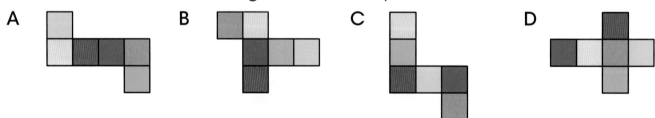

A   B   C   D

Which arrangement **cannot** be folded to make a cube?

2   Here is an open top box in the shape of a cube.
    The box was made from this net.

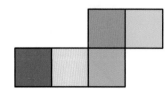

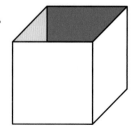

Draw the net. Mark the net to show which square is the base of the cube.
Use an X to mark the square.

3 Below is a page torn from Mikela's notebook.

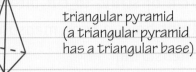

Pyramids
- A pyramid is a 3D shape.
- The base is a polygon.
- The other faces are triangles which meet at a point called the apex or vertex.

square pyramid
(a square pyramid has a square base)

Examples of pyramids
- A tetrahedron is a triangular pyramid ...

triangular pyramid
(a triangular pyramid has a triangular base)

Use Mikela's notes to help you finish off the description of a tetrahedron.

Use the words 'faces', 'edges' and 'vertices' to describe a tetrahedron.

4 Here are the nets of six 3D shapes. One of them will **not** make a pyramid.
Work with a partner to identify each shape, then describe its properties.

(a)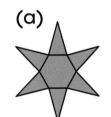
(b)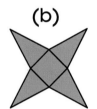
(c)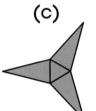
(d)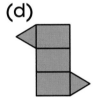
(e)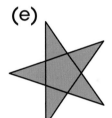
(f)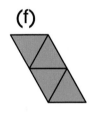

5 Lydia is thinking of a 3D shape. What shape is Lydia thinking of?

My shape has 5 faces. The two opposite faces are triangles. The other 3 faces are rectangles.

6 Here are some shapes made from regular triangles.
Which shapes will fold to make a pyramid with a solid base?

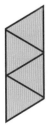

A

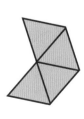
B

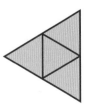
C

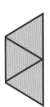
D

Measure

Measuring length

Let's investigate

I had 90 cm of string to cut into three equal lengths, but I did not have a tape measure. I cut the string without measuring.

When I measured the pieces later, I found that one piece was exactly the right length, but a second piece was twice the length of the third piece. What lengths were my pieces of string?

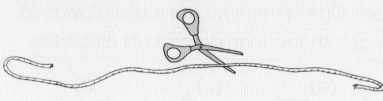

Vocabulary

m: metre, a standard measure of length.

cm: centimetre, one hundredth of a metre.

mm: millimetre, one thousandth of a metre.

1 m = 100 cm = 1000 mm

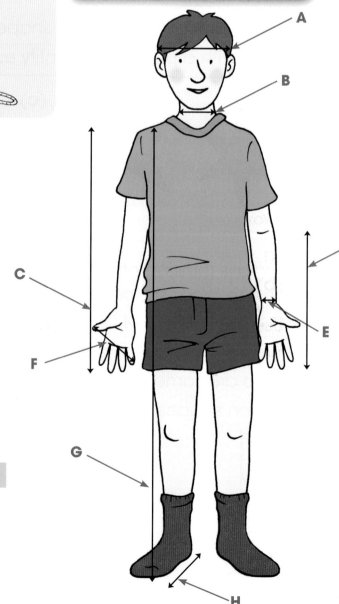

1   Work with a partner to record the measurements of their body parts. Copy the list below.

Check that your partner is using the measuring equipment correctly and reading the scale accurately.

   A.   Head circumference   **?**
   B.   Neck circumference   **?**
   C.   Shoulder to fingertips   **?**
   D.   Elbow to fingertips   **?**
   E.   Wrist circumference   **?**
   F.   Handspan   **?**
   G.   Height from ground to shoulder   **?**
   H.   Foot length   **?**

2   Is Parveen correct?

The length of a person's foot is the same as their measurement from elbow to wrist.

Explain how you would investigate whether this statement is always true, sometimes true or never true.

3   Daniela, Natalia and Sebastian have been travelling around South America. On their travels they have observed the height of some of the trees.

Tree	Height
Acacia	850 cm
Brazilian Walnut	3450 cm
Cashew	1130 cm
Chilean Myrtle	1310 cm
Fig tree	1260 cm
Jacaranda	980 cm
Mistol	620 cm
Quebracho	2270 cm
Tamarind	1500 cm
Wax palm	1840 cm

(a) Order the trees from shortest to tallest.

(b) Change the measurements from centimetres to metres.

Use the order to check that you have converted from cm to m correctly. To help you, you could copy this table and complete it.

Order	Tree	Height in metres
Shortest		
…		
…		
…		
Tallest		

Telling the time (2)

Let's investigate

I looked at the clock reflected in the mirror when I left the house. I looked at the clock in the mirror again when I got home. How long have I been out of the house?

The time when I left the house.

The time when I got home.

Try looking at the pictures in a mirror. Then use a timeline to solve the problem.

1   You have to be home by 3 o'clock. You look at your watch six times during the day.

Time problems can be worked out using a timeline. For example, the time from 1:45 to 3:00 is 1 hour and 15 minutes:

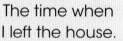

15 mins   1 hour

1:45   2:00   3:00

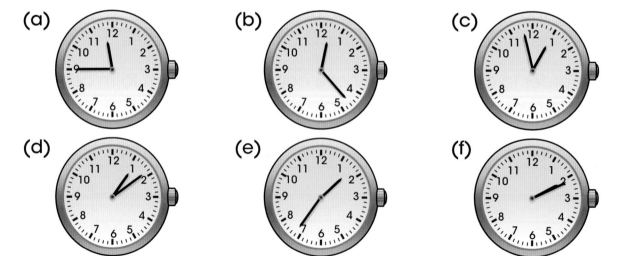

For each time that you check your watch, calculate how much time you have left before you should be home.

74

2 Martin dropped his digital clock. When he picked it up he could not tell which way up it was! Write in words the two times it could be.

3 Later he looked at the clock and knew exactly what the time was. Why was that?

4 Write down three different times that look the same on a digital clock whichever way up it is.

5 Next day, Martin saw this time on the clock. He knew exactly what the time was. Why was that?

6 Match the watches to the children.

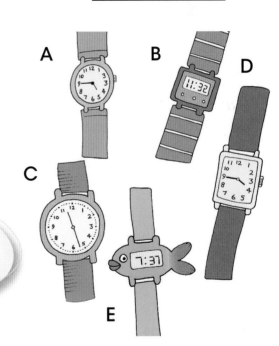

1 My watch should read 20 to 12, but it is 8 minutes slow.

2 My watch should read 25 to 8, but it is 2 minutes fast.

3 My watch should read a quarter past 4, but it is half an hour slow.

4 My watch should say 4:40, but it is 5 minutes fast.

5 My watch should read 17 minutes past 11 but it is 10 minutes fast.

Using calendars

Let's investigate

If the last day of the month is a Sunday, what day might the 1st day of the month have been?

> How many days is it possible to have in one month? You could use a blank calendar to help investigage the problem. There is more than one answer!

Vocabulary

calendar: table showing the days of the week and months of the year.

date: a record that tells you the day, month and year.

1 This is part of a family calendar.

March	Mother	Father	Leila	Anya	Gina
Monday 1	meeting 11 am			spelling test 10 am	
Tuesday 2		dentist 10 am	ballet 5:30 pm		
Wednesday 3					ballet 4:30 pm
Thursday 4	parents meet teachers 6 pm	parents meet teachers 6 pm			optician 4 pm
Friday 5			after-school maths club	gymnastics 4:15 pm	
Saturday 6			party 6 pm		
Sunday 7					

(a) What is Leila doing on Friday?

(b) When is Father's dentist appointment?

(c) Who has a ballet lesson on Wednesday?

(d) Which day of the week does Anya go to gymnastics?

(e) Who is Mother with on Thursday evening?

(f) Gina wants to visit a friend after school. Which days is she free?

2   This calendar has been splattered with ink.

September					
Mon		7	14	21	28
Tue	1	8	15	22	29
Wed	2	9	16	23	30
Thu	3	10	17	24	
Fri	4	11	18	25	
Sat	5	12	19	26	
Sun	6	13	20	27	

October				
Mon		5		26
Tue		6		
Wed				
Thu	1			
Fri	2			
Sat	3	10	1	
Sun	4	11	18.	

November					
Mon		2	9	16	23	30
Tue		3	10	17	24	
Wed		4	11	25		
Thu		5		26		
Fri		6		27		
Sat		7		21	28	
Sun	1	8	15	22	29	

December					
Mon		7	14	21	28
Tue	1	8	15	22	29
Wed	2	9	16	23	30
Thu	3	10	17		
Fri	4	11	18		
Sat	5	12			
Sun	6		27		

Work with a partner and use your knowledge
of calendars to answer the questions below.

(a) On what day of the week is 18 November?

(b) On what day of the week is 8 October?

(c) Sofie is going to have a party on a Saturday
    in December. Which dates could she choose?

(d) How many Mondays are there in October?

(e) Bruno's birthday is 24 November.
    What is the date of the Sunday closest to his birthday?

(f) What day is the last day in December?

(g) What is the date of the second Tuesday in October?

(h) The date is 15 October. How long is it until 25 December?

When the time gap is
more than 7 days,
record it as weeks
and days.
For example: 17 days
= 2 weeks and 3 days.

Area (2)

Let's investigate

Jen is digging a vegetable patch. The patch is $47\,m^2$. She can dig $4\,m^2$ every day. How many days will it take her to dig the whole patch?

1   Francesco is designing a herb garden. Each square on his plan represents 1 square metre.

square centimetre (cm^2): 1 square centimetre is a unit of measure where the length is 1 cm and the width is 1 cm.

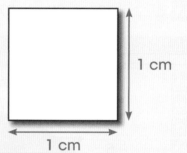

1 cm

1 cm

square metre (m^2): 1 square metre is a unit of measure where the length is 1 m and the width is 1 m.

(a) What is the total area of Francesco's herb garden?

(b) One quarter of the whole herb garden is for rosemary. What size area is that?

(c) $3\,m^2$ of the herb garden is for thyme. What fraction of the total area is that?

(d) Copy the grid. Design a herb garden with $4\,m^2$ rosemary, $3\,m^2$ thyme, $3\,m^2$ sage, $2\,m^2$ basil, $2\,m^2$ mint, $1\,m^2$ tarragon and $1\,m^2$ fennel.

2 Each small square represents $1\,cm^2$.
Find the areas of the rectangles A, B and C.

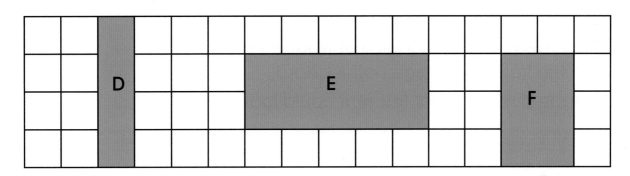

3 Each small square represents $1\,cm^2$. Calculate the area covered by each each rectangle.

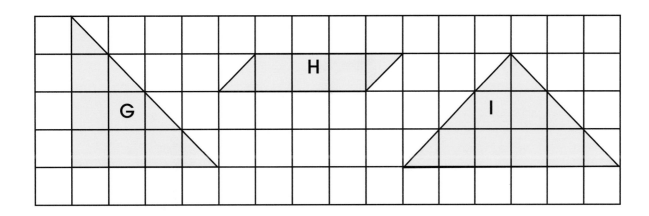

4 Each small square represents $1\,cm^2$. Work out the area of these shapes by counting the squares.

Pair up half-squares to make whole centimetre squares.

Perimeter (2)

Vocabulary

perimeter: the distance around a shape.

Let's investigate

A rectangle has a perimeter of 30 cm.
What could be the length of its sides?
Find all the possible answers in whole centimetre lengths.

?

?

?

?

Remember the properties of rectangles. Work in an ordered way so that you will know when you have all the solutions.

1   Alice has twelve 1-metre lengths of wooden sticks to make the frame of a large noticeboard.

   If she made a rectangular frame, it could look like this:

   5 metres

   1 metre **1 metre**

   5 metres

   (a) There are other rectangular frames that could be made using 12 m of wooden sticks.

   Write down the measurements of two possible rectangles.

   If Alice made a frame that was not rectangular, it could look like this:

   All the lengths of this shape are 1 metre.

   (b) What could be the shapes of two other frames that are not rectangular?

2   Measure the perimeter of each of these rectangles
    in millimetres (mm).

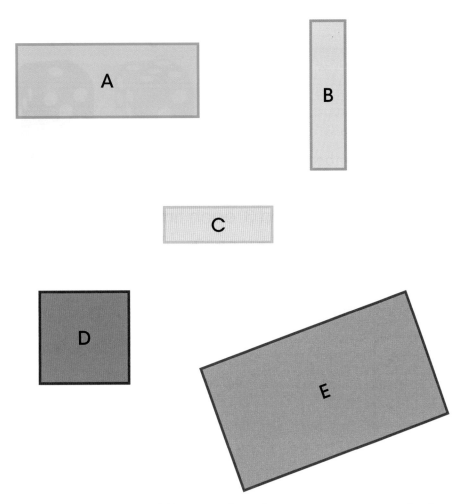

3   Convert each of the perimeter measurements from question 2
    into centimetres (cm).

4   You need to measure the perimeter of the rectangle below, but
    the corner has been broken off.

    Work with a partner. Discuss how you might be able to work out
    the perimeter of the rectangle before the corner was broken.

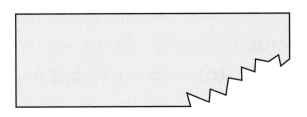

Number

Special numbers

Let's investigate

Three dice are arranged in a row so that only odd numbers can be seen on top.

How many different ways can the dice be arranged so that they show only odd numbers on top?

1   5   1

1   The rule for a sequence of numbers is 'add 3' each time.   2, 5, 8, 11, 14 …
    Which of these numbers belong to the sequence?
    23   29   34   38   41   46

2   Mira shaded some numbers on a number square.

1	2	3	4	5	6
7	8	9	10	11	12
13	14	15	16	17	18
19	20	21	22	23	24
25	26	27	28	29	30
31	32	33	34	35	36

(a) The numbers form a pattern.
    What is the rule for finding the next number?

(b) What would be the next number in this pattern?

3   Explain the rule for each sequence in words.
    (a) 1, 4, 7, 10, 13 …   (b) 8, 6, 4, 2, 0 …   (c) −15, −10, −5, 0, 5 …
    (d) 10, 7, 4, 1, −2 …   (e) −3, 1, 5, 9 …

4 Here is the start of a sequence of numbers. 1, ? , ? …

Make up your own rule and complete the sequence.
Write down the rule you have used.

Choose another rule. Complete the sequence again and write down
the rule you have used. Now show your sequences to your partner.
Can they work out the rules?

5 Copy the diagram.

Write the numbers 1, 2, 3, 4 and 5 in the circles so that the
total of the row is the same as the total of the column.

(a) How many different ways can you find?

(b) What do you notice about the number in the centre?

6 Copy the Carroll diagram.

	less than 20	not less than 20
odd		
not odd		

Write each of these numbers in the correct place on the sorting diagram.

13   18   25   35   42

7 Here are three word cards.

Which card would you choose to complete
each of these sentences?

(a) When you add two even numbers together the answer is …

(b) When you subtract an odd number from an even number
the answer is …

(c) When you add three odd numbers together the answer is …

8 Write an example to match each of the general statements below.

(a) The sum of an odd number and an even number is an odd number.

(b) The sum of three odd numbers is odd.

(c) Any odd number is double a number plus 1.

(d) Any odd number is double a number subtract 1.

(e) The difference between two odd numbers is even.

Exploring fractions

Let's investigate

Use digits from 1 to 10 to make as many pairs of equivalent fractions as you can.

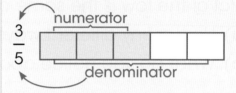

Try using number cards, for example:

$$\frac{1}{2} = \frac{2}{4} \qquad \frac{1}{2} = \frac{3}{6}$$

Vocabulary

numerator: the top number of a fraction; it tells us how many parts we have.

denominator: the bottom number of a fraction; it tells us how many equal parts a whole has been divided into.

$$\frac{3}{5}$$

numerator

denominator

equivalent fractions: fractions that are the same size.

$$\frac{2}{4}$$

$$\frac{1}{2}$$

$$\frac{2}{4} = \frac{1}{2}$$

1 Look at the fraction wall.

1 whole											
$\frac{1}{2}$						$\frac{1}{2}$					
$\frac{1}{3}$				$\frac{1}{3}$				$\frac{1}{3}$			
$\frac{1}{4}$			$\frac{1}{4}$			$\frac{1}{4}$			$\frac{1}{4}$		
$\frac{1}{6}$		$\frac{1}{6}$		$\frac{1}{6}$		$\frac{1}{6}$		$\frac{1}{6}$		$\frac{1}{6}$	
$\frac{1}{12}$	$\frac{1}{12}$	$\frac{1}{12}$	$\frac{1}{12}$	$\frac{1}{12}$	$\frac{1}{12}$	$\frac{1}{12}$	$\frac{1}{12}$	$\frac{1}{12}$	$\frac{1}{12}$	$\frac{1}{12}$	$\frac{1}{12}$

Use the fraction wall to help you complete these equivalent fractions.

(a) $\frac{1}{2} = \frac{?}{6}$

(b) $\frac{1}{2} = \frac{?}{12}$

(c) $\frac{1}{3} = \frac{?}{6}$

(d) $\frac{2}{3} = \frac{?}{12}$

(e) $\frac{3}{4} = \frac{?}{12}$

(f) $\frac{5}{6} = \frac{?}{12}$

2 Find four pairs of equivalent fractions on the grid.
Which fraction is left over?

$\frac{8}{10}$	$\frac{7}{10}$	$\frac{3}{10}$
$\frac{1}{2}$	$\frac{4}{5}$	$\frac{4}{10}$
$\frac{5}{10}$	$\frac{35}{50}$	$\frac{30}{100}$

3 Copy the spider diagram shown below.
Complete it so that opposite fractions add to 1.

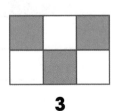

Write out number sentences to help you.

$$\frac{1}{2} + \frac{?}{?} = 1$$

4 Look at these shapes. One of the shapes matches
all the descriptions below. Which one is it?

- Part of the shape is shaded.
- The shape is not a circle.
- The shape is not divided into fifths.
- The shape is divided into equal parts.
- More than one third of the shape is shaded.

1

2

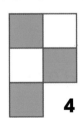

3

4

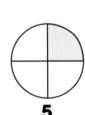

5

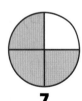

6

7

8

5 Complete the number statements using one of these signs: =, < or >.

(a) $\frac{3}{4}$ **?** $\frac{17}{20}$ (b) $\frac{7}{9}$ **?** $\frac{28}{36}$ (c) $\frac{1}{4}$ **?** $\frac{1}{3}$

6 Complete these number calculations.

(a) $\frac{1}{4}$ + **?** = 1   (b) $\frac{3}{4}$ + **?** = 1   (c) $\frac{2}{5}$ + $\frac{3}{5}$ = **?**

Fractions, decimals and mixed numbers

Let's investigate

Each cloud contains the digits from a fraction and its equivalent decimal. The digits have been mixed up.

Write the fraction and equivalent decimal for each cloud.

Here is one I did earlier.

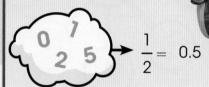

$\frac{1}{2} = 0.5$

1 Look at the number line.

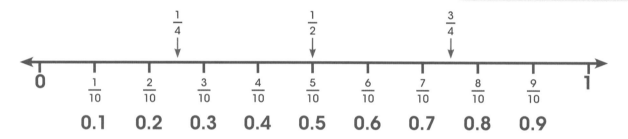

Use the number line to help you find the larger number in each of these pairs:

(a) 0.3 and 0.5

(b) 0.2 and $\frac{1}{2}$

(c) 0.25 and $\frac{1}{2}$

(d) 0.6 and $\frac{1}{2}$

(e) $\frac{1}{4}$ and 0.4

(f) 1 and 0.9

(g) 0.5 and 0.25

(h) 0.8 and $\frac{1}{4}$

2 This table shows a fraction and its equivalent decimal.

Copy the table and complete it.

Fraction	Decimal
$\frac{1}{10}$	?
?	0.75
$\frac{1}{4}$	?
?	0.6

3 Look at the set of fractions and decimals.

Which ones are **greater** than $\frac{1}{2}$?

0.55 $\frac{6}{8}$ 0.7   0.34 $\frac{3}{4}$ $\frac{3}{6}$ 0.45

4 Which **two** fractions are equivalent to 0.7?

$\dfrac{7}{10}$ $\dfrac{1}{70}$ $\dfrac{70}{100}$ $\dfrac{1}{7}$

5 This diagram represents the mixed number $1\dfrac{1}{3}$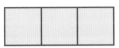

Look at these diagrams. Write each as a mixed number.

    (a)   **(b)**   **(c)**

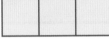

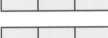

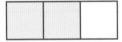

6 Which mixed numbers go in the boxes marked A, B and C?

7 Draw a number line like this one.

0   **5**

(a) Draw an arrow (⬆) at $1\dfrac{1}{2}$ on your number line.

(b) Draw an arrow (⬆) at $3\dfrac{1}{4}$ on your number line.

8 Order the following set of fractions and decimals.
Start with the smallest number.

2.1   3.4 $1\dfrac{1}{2}$ 3.6 $3\dfrac{1}{4}$

Fractions of ...

Let's investigate

Saima is thinking of a number.

> One third of my number is 9.

Check your answer.

If you divide it by 3 are you left with 9?

What number is Saima thinking of?

1   Copy this diagram.

Find the missing numbers.

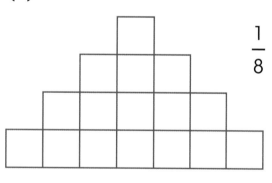

$\frac{1}{4}$ of 24 = **?**

$\frac{1}{3}$ of 24 = **?**

24

$\frac{1}{8}$ of 24 = **?**

$\frac{1}{2}$ of 24 = **?**

2   Copy these diagrams. Colour in the requested fraction.

(a)

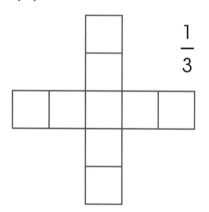

$\frac{1}{3}$

(b)

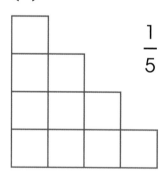

$\frac{1}{5}$

(c)

$\frac{1}{8}$

3   What fraction of these squares is shaded?

(a)

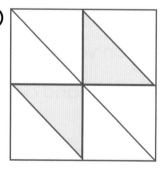

(b)

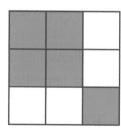

4 Work out the following.

(a) $\frac{1}{3}$ of 18   (b) $\frac{1}{4}$ of 16   (c) $\frac{1}{5}$ of 35

5 What is $\frac{1}{3}$ of $12?

6 These diagrams are made of squares.

Which ones have exactly $\frac{1}{3}$ shaded?

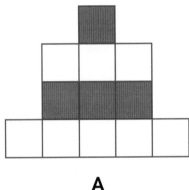
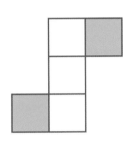
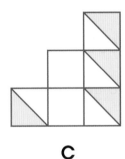

A   **B**   **C**

7 Sanjiv has six T-shirts.

What fraction of Sanjiv's T-shirts are plain white?

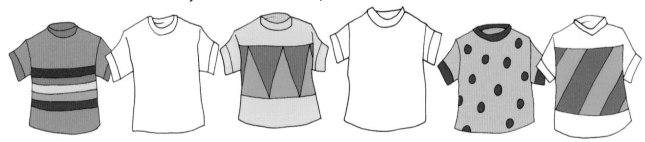

8 What are the missing fractions?

(a) 24 ÷ 3 is equivalent to **?** of 24

(b) 16 ÷ 8 is equivalent to **?** of 16

9 Which would you choose $\frac{1}{3}$ of $15, or $\frac{1}{4}$ of $16? Explain your answer.

10 Here is a chocolate bar.

Roz eats 3 pieces and Selina eats 5 pieces.

What fraction of the chocolate bar remains?

Write the fraction in its simplest form.

Ratio and proportion

Let's investigate

How tall do you think the cactus is?

The person is 160 cm tall.

Now how tall do you think the cactus is?

Vocabulary

in every: 1 in every 4 squares is grey.

for every: for every grey square, there are 3 white squares.

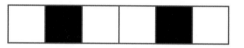

part: fraction of a whole.

1. 1 in every 3 squares in this pattern is black. The pattern continues in the same way.

   Copy and complete this table.

White squares	Black squares
8	?
?	6
14	?

2. Saif makes green paint by mixing yellow paint with blue paint. He uses 2 cans of yellow paint for every 1 can of blue paint.

   Saif uses 8 cans of yellow paint to make enough green paint to decorate his bedroom.

   How many cans of blue paint does he use?

3 A picture of a toy is one fifth the size of the real toy.

The toy is 5cm high in the picture.

How high is the real toy?

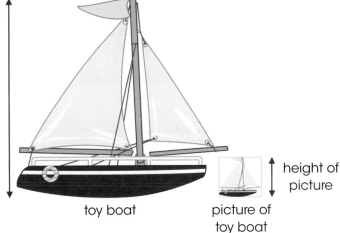

5 × height of picture

height of picture

toy boat

picture of toy boat

4 Zara is making sauce. She uses 5 tomatoes for every 1 litre of sauce.

(a) How many litres of sauce can she make from 15 tomatoes?

(b) How many tomatoes does she need for 2 litres of sauce?

5 Here is a bead pattern. For every 1 purple bead, there are 4 green beads.

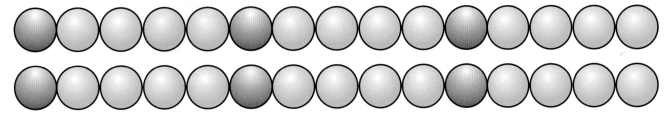

Draw bead patterns to match these descriptions:

(a) For every 1 black bead, 3 beads are white.

(b) In every 3 beads, 1 is white.

6 Here is a recipe to make 12 gingerbread men.

Work out how much flour, butter and sugar are needed to make 24 gingerbread men.

Copy and complete the table shown below.

350 grams flour
125 grams butter
175 grams brown sugar
4 tablespoons syrup
8 teaspoons ginger

	flour	butter	sugar
24 gingerbread men	?	?	?

Measure

Measuring capacity

Let's investigate

I had a 900 ml jug of juice.

I poured all of the juice into 5 glasses.

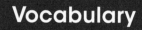

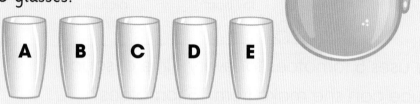

Half of the juice was shared equally between glass A and glass B.

The other half of the juice was shared equally between glasses C, D and E.

How much juice was in each glass?

Start by working out half of 900 ml.

1 These drinks are sold in 1 litre bottles. Each bottle must be full.
   Work out how much is needed of the last ingredient for each drink.

Strawberry Sparkle

Strawberry Juice 230ml

Apple juice 350ml

Lemonade

Melon Medley

Melon Juice 460ml

Mango juice 280ml

Apple Juice

Pear fizz

Pear juice 360ml

Apple juice 240ml

Lemonade

Banana Cream

Mashed Bananas 560ml

Milk 350ml

Sugar Syrup

Tropical Breeze

Guava 270ml

Pineapple 380ml

Papaya

Starry Night

Star fruit 480ml

Melon juice 480ml

Lime juice

2 Look carefully at the measuring cylinder.

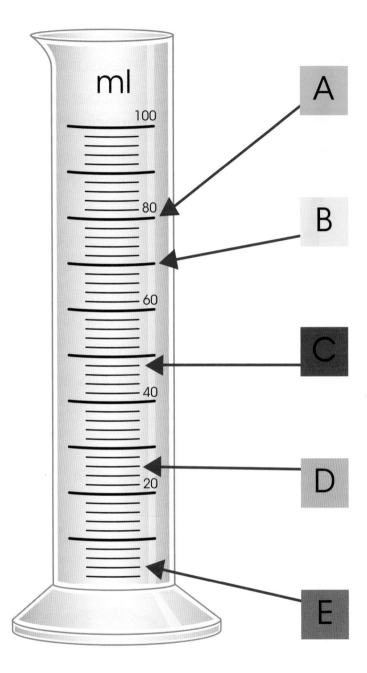

(a) How much does each large line on the scale show?

(b) How much does each small line on the scale show?

(c) Read the scale for the points shown by the arrows.

Capacity, length and mass

Let's investigate

Simone had a pencil measuring 16 cm long and it weighed 4 grams.

Beatrice had a similar pencil, and hers measured 8 cm. How much do you think it weighed?

Nicole also had a similar pencil. It weighed 3 g. How long do you think it was?

Vocabulary

m: metre, a standard measure of length.

cm: centimetre, one hundredth of a metre.

mm: millimetre, one thousandth of a metre.

g: gram, a standard measure of mass.

mg: milligram, one thousandth of a gram.

kg: kilogram, 1000 grams.

1 Class 4 have been doing lots of measuring. Here are some of the things they have measured.

Each object had a label showing the measurement that Class 4 had made, but the labels fell off.

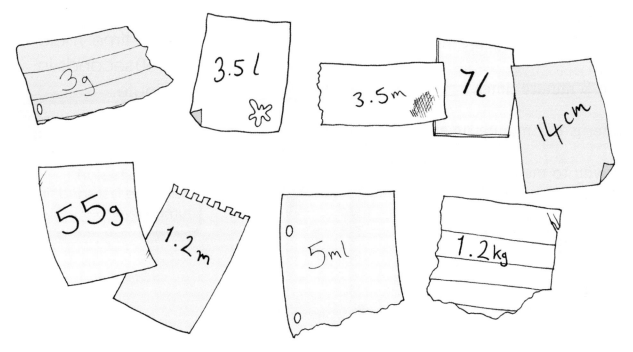

With a partner, work out which label went with each object.

Height of the bookcase = **?**

Capacity of the saucepan = **?**

Sophie's hand span = **?**

Weight of the globe = **?**

Capacity of a teaspoon = **?**

Weight of a chess piece = **?**

Length of string = **?**

Capacity of a washing up bowl = **?**

Weight of a hair brush = **?**

2   Choose one of these questions and plan how you would investigate it with a partner or group.

(a) What length of string weighs 10 g?

(b) How much water weighs 200 g?

(c) How much water do you have to put into a bucket for it to measure 10 cm deep?

Measuring time

Let's investigate

You have two sand timers.

One is a 5 minute timer.

The other is a 7 minute timer.

Find a way to measure:

12 minutes, 15 minutes, 2 minutes, 9 minutes and 3 minutes.

second: a standard unit of time. There are 60 seconds in 1 minute.

The timing does not have to start when the first sand timer is turned over.

1   With a partner, use a timer to find out:

   (a) How long it takes to write your name 10 times.

   (b) How long it takes to say the alphabet backwards.

   (c) How long it takes to say the 9× table.

2   Six children have run a 100 m sprint race.

Name	Time in seconds
Leah	16
Isobel	15
Natasha	13
Bethan	18
Anya	17
Charlotte	15

(a) Who won the race?

(b) Write the names in order of where the girls came in the race. Start with the fastest.

(c) How many seconds faster was Charlotte than Bethan?

3   These clocks all show the wrong time.
    What time should each clock show?
    Answer using digital clock notation:

(a)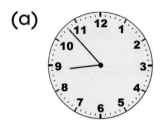

This clock is 10 minutes slow.

(b)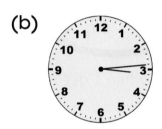

This clock is 5 minutes fast.

(c)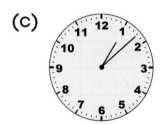

This clock is 15 minutes fast.

(d)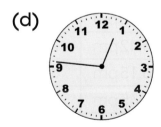

This clock is half an hour slow.

Calculating time

Let's investigate

I looked at the clock reflected in the mirror when I left the house. I looked at the clock in the mirror again when I got home. What were the real times?

Try looking at the pictures in a mirror.

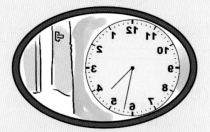

The time when I left the house.   The time when I get home.

Sunday	Ourtown – Newcity				
	Bus A	**Bus B**	**Bus C**	**Bus D**	**Bus E**	**Bus F**
Ourtown	9:18 am	10:38 am	12:28 pm	2:18 pm	3:38 pm	5:28 pm
Riverton	9:53 am	11:13 am	1:03 pm	2:53 pm	4:13 pm	6:03 pm
Hillbury	10:23 am	11:43 am	1:33 pm	3:23 pm	4:43 pm	6:33 pm
Colville	10:56 am	12:16 pm	2:06 pm	3:56 pm	5:16 pm	7:06 pm
Newcity	11:38 am	12:58 pm	2:48 pm	4:38 pm	5:58 pm	7:48 pm

Sunday	Newcity – Ourtown				
	Bus G	**Bus H**	**Bus I**	**Bus J**	**Bus K**	**Bus L**
Newcity	10:40 am	12:00 pm	1:50 pm	3:40 pm	5:00 pm	6:50 pm
Colville	11:22 am	12:42 pm	2:32 pm	4:22 pm	5:42 pm	7:32 pm
Hillbury	11:55 am	1:15 pm	3:05 pm	4:55 pm	6:15 pm	8:05 pm
Riverton	12:25 pm	1:45 pm	3:35 pm	5:25 pm	6:45 pm	8:35 pm
Ourtown	1:00 pm	2:20 pm	4:10 pm	6:00 pm	7:20 pm	9:10 pm

1   Michael lives in Riverton. He is visiting his aunt in Newcity this Sunday. He wants to see his aunt for at least 2 hours and get home before 7 pm. At which different times might he catch buses?

2 At his aunt's house, Michael looks at his watch.

How long will it be until the next bus leaves Newcity?

3 Michael decided to catch Bus K on the way home.
He looks at his watch again.

How long will it be before he gets to his stop?

4 The bus company are planning another bus from Newcity to Ourtown.
It will leave Newcity at 9:50 am. If it takes the same time to do the
journey as the other buses, when will it arrive at each stop?

Area and perimeter

Let's investigate

This rectangle has been made from 1 cm squares. The end has broken off.

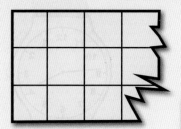

Draw **three** different rectangles that might have been this rectangle before it was broken.

The rectangle must have a width of 3 cm. The length must be at least 4 cm.

Label each rectangle with the area and perimeter.

1   Area Puzzle

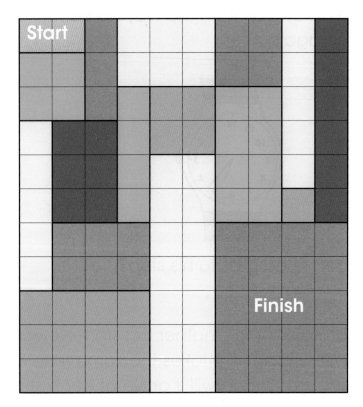

(a) Start on the orange rectangle at the top left.

Move through the design from rectangle to rectangle so that the next rectangle you move to has an area larger than the previous one.

Find a path through the rectangles that finishes at the purple rectangle at the bottom right.

(b) Is it possible to find a path by only moving to rectangles with a longer perimeter than the previous one?

2 These are the first three shapes in a sequence.
The shapes are made using 1 cm squares.

1st   **2nd**   **3rd**

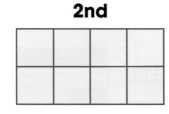

(a) Describe how the shape is changing.

(b) Draw the 4th and 5th shapes in the sequence.

(c) For each shape work out the perimeter and area. Copy and complete the table.

(d) Predict what the area and perimeter for the 6th shape might be.
Draw the 6th shape to check.

Shape	Area	Perimeter
1st	6 cm²	10 cm
2nd		
3rd		
4th		
5th		

3 Each of these shapes is a square with one 1 cm square missing from the corner.

1st   **2nd**   **3rd**

 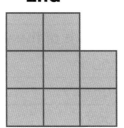 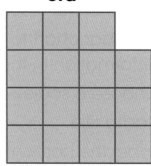

(a) Describe how the shape is changing.

(b) Draw the 4th and 5th shapes in the sequence.

(c) For each shape work out the perimeter and area. Copy and complete the table.

(d) Predict what the area and perimeter for the 6th shape might be.
Draw the 6th shape to check.

Shape	Area	Perimeter
1st	3 cm²	8 cm
2nd		
3rd		
4th		
5th		

Handling data

Bar charts

Let's investigate

Look at the graph and the labels. Explain which three labels could be used for the title and axes of the graph and why.

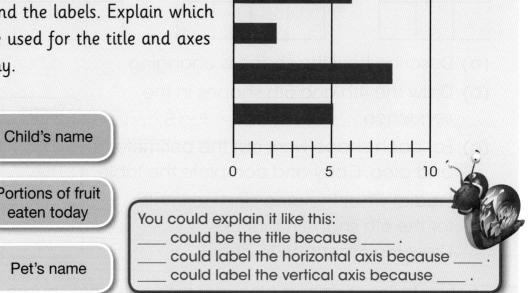

Height in metres (m)

Child's name

Number of pieces of fruit

Portions of fruit eaten today

Number of pets

Pet's name

You could explain it like this:
_____ could be the title because _____ .
_____ could label the horizontal axis because _____ .
_____ could label the vertical axis because _____ .

1 Laila found out when everyone's birthdays were in her school. This is a table of her results.

(a) Make a bar chart to show the information in the table.

 • Choose a scale.

 • Add a title.

 • Label the horizontal axis and vertical axis.

(b) Compare your graph with other learners' graphs. Did you choose the same scale? If not, which scale is clearer and why?

Month of the year	Number of birthdays
January	20
February	16
March	28
April	27
May	18
June	31
July	29
August	14
September	15
October	15
November	10
December	22

2 Fatima wondered whether the birthdays in her class had a similar pattern to the whole school. She made this graph. Make a table of the information in the graph.

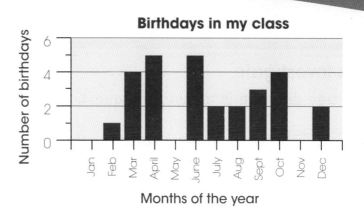

3 Jug A contains 2 litres of water. Jug B contains 1 litre. During the day, the amount of water in the jugs changes. Sometimes people pour some water from a jug, sometimes they refill a jug. Class 4 recorded how much water was in the two jugs every 10 minutes.

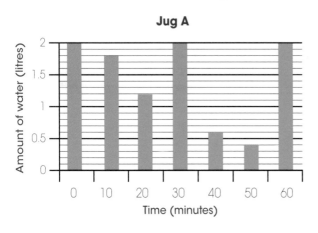

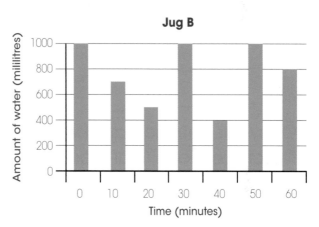

The graphs use different scales. This makes it difficult to compare the amounts of water in each jug. Draw the graph for Jug B again, but use the same scale as the graph for Jug A. Your new graph will show the amount of water measured in litres.

4 Answer these questions, using **your** graph for Jug B and the graph for Jug A:

(a) How much water was in Jug A at 40 minutes?

(b) How much water was in Jug B at 40 minutes?

(c) After they started measuring, how many times was each jug refilled?

(d) How much more water was in Jug A than Jug B at 60 minutes?

(e) How much water was in the jugs altogether at 20 minutes?

(f) After how many minutes were they closest to having no water?

Tree diagrams

Let's investigate

This tree diagram is missing the question text.

What questions could have sorted these numbers?

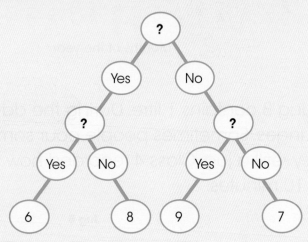

Vocabulary

frequency table: a table used to record data.

tree diagram or **branching database:** a diagram shaped so that each 'branch' shows a possible outcome.

What do the two numbers on the left have in common?
How are they different from the two numbers on the right?
There is more than one answer!

1   Copy this tree diagram. Draw and name a shape at the end of each final branch.

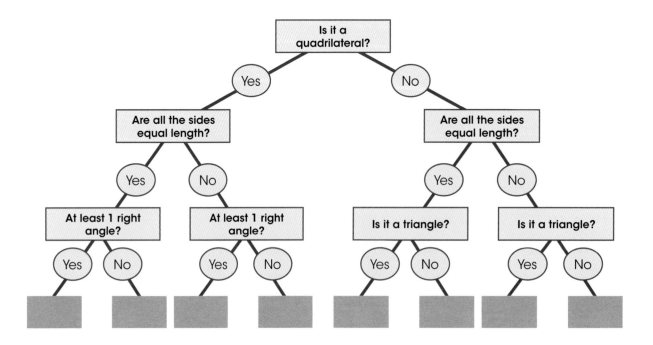

2 Write questions to sort these shapes using a tree diagram.

To sort the 3D shapes think about:
• the number of faces
• the shapes of the faces
• the number of edges
• the number of vertices.

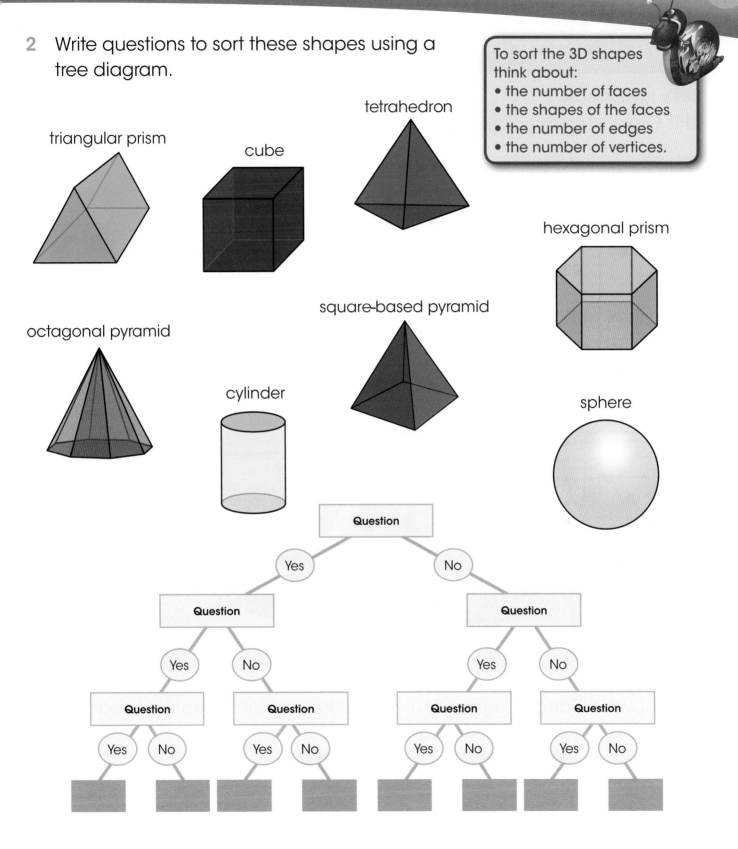

tetrahedron

triangular prism

cube

hexagonal prism

octagonal pyramid

square-based pyramid

cylinder

sphere

Extra challenge: try to think of questions that sort the shapes so that the 'Yes' and 'No' groups are the same size, so that you have one shape in each grey box.

Let's investigate

This Carroll diagram has missing labels. What might they be?

Copy the Carroll diagram. Complete it by adding correct labels.

		not
	225 985 755 405	900 370 220 810
not	873 669 111 557	444 202 998 556

> Look to see what all the numbers in each row and column have in common. Use what you know about times tables.

1   Imagine you are a scientist observing alien creatures on a far away world.

Copy the Carroll diagram. Draw an imaginary alien creature in each section of your Carroll diagram.

	purple	not purple
3 eyes		
not 3 eyes		

2 Copy this blank Carroll diagram.

Choose your own categories and draw four more imaginary aliens that fit your categories.

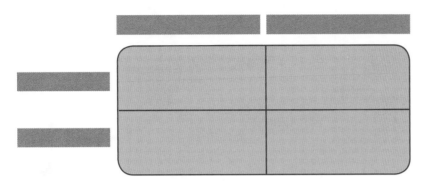

3 **(a)** Copy the Carroll diagram below.

	less than $\frac{3}{4}$	not less than $\frac{3}{4}$
equivalent to $\frac{1}{2}$		
not equivalent to $\frac{1}{2}$		

Complete your diagram by placing these fractions and decimals in the correct sections.

> 0.1 $\frac{7}{8}$ $\frac{1}{3}$ $\frac{3}{4}$ $\frac{5}{10}$ $\frac{4}{10}$ $\frac{1}{4}$ 0.8
>
> 0.9 $\frac{2}{4}$ $\frac{7}{10}$ 0.3 $\frac{4}{8}$ 0.5

(b) Write a sentence to explain why one of the sections of the Carroll diagram is empty.

You could start your sentence with: *"It is impossible to ..."*

Venn diagrams (2)

Let's investigate

There are 25 children in the class.

12 children in the class like strawberry ice cream.

Of these 12 children, 5 also like vanilla ice cream.

2 children do not like either flavour.

How many children altogether like vanilla ice cream?

Copy the Venn diagram and use it to solve the problem.

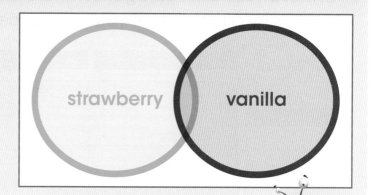

Write the numbers in the spaces in your Venn diagram. Check that the numbers make the statements in the problem true.

1   This is a fashion designer's Venn diagram.
    Each circle represents a colour for an outfit.

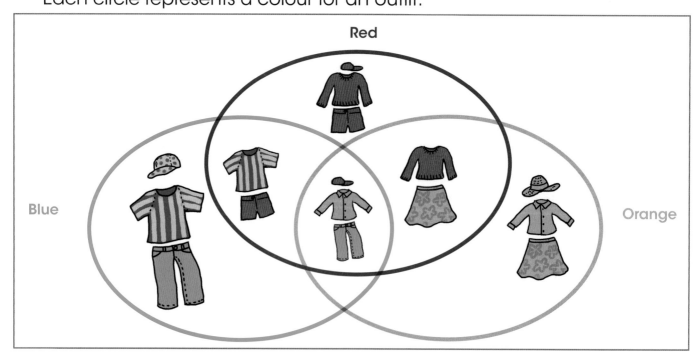

Copy the Venn diagram but choose **your own** colours.

In each section, draw an outfit. In the centre, draw an outfit with one item of each colour.

2 Look at this Venn diagram.

The green circle for 'multiples of 6' is inside the blue circle for 'multiples of 2'. This is because all multiples of 6 are also in the 2 times table. But there are some numbers inside the blue circle but outside the green circle. This is because not all the multiples of 2 are in the 6 times table, for example 2 and 28.

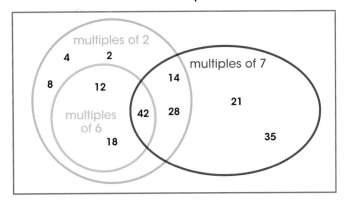

Numbers have been written in each section of the diagram.
Check that the numbers are in the correct places.

3 Draw these Venn diagrams and write two numbers in each section. Don't forget that the area outside of the hoops is also a section of the Venn diagram.

(a)

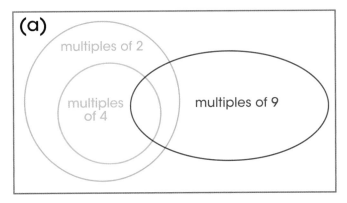

(b)

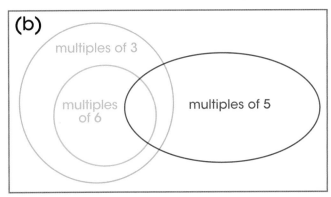

(c)

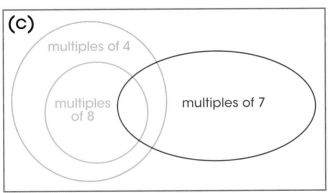

(d)

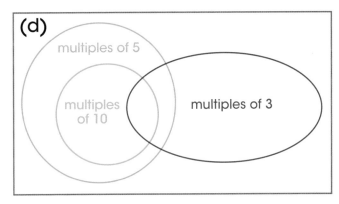